WILD FIRE

The Culture, Science, and Future of Fire

FERIN DAVIS ANDERSON
and STEPHANIE SAMMARTINO MCPHERSON

TWENTY-FIRST CENTURY BOOKS / MINNEAPOLIS

To my family and to the fire keepers and knowledge holders, who have always kindled the fire within us. **—F.D.A.**

For my husband, and our daughters and sons-in-law, Jennifer and Wayne and Marianne and Daniel. **—S.S.M.**

First paperback edition published in 2025

Twenty-First Century Books™
An imprint of Lerner Publishing Group, Inc.
241 First Avenue North
Minneapolis, MN 55401 USA

For reading levels and more information, look up this title at www.lernerbooks.com.

Main body text set in Adobe Garamond Pro.
Typeface provided by Adobe Systems.

Library of Congress Cataloging-in-Publication Data

Names: Anderson, Ferin Davis, author. | McPherson, Stephanie Sammartino, author.
Title: Wildfire : the culture, science, and future of fire / Ferin Davis Anderson, Stephanie Sammartino McPherson.
Description: Minneapolis : Twenty-First Century Books, [2024] | Includes bibliographical references and index. | Audience: Ages 13–18 | Audience: Grades 10–12 | Summary: "Environmental scientist Ferin Anderson and author Stephanie Sammartino McPherson examine how Indigenous people, farmers, and forestry departments have used fire to manage resources and how climate change is impacting the future of fire"— Provided by publisher.
Identifiers: LCCN 2023036389 (print) | LCCN 2023036390 (ebook) | ISBN 9781728424002 (library binding) | ISBN 9798765602317 (epub)
Subjects: LCSH: Wildfires—Juvenile literature. | BISAC: YOUNG ADULT NONFICTION / Science & Nature / Environmental Science & Ecosystems
Classification: LCC SD421.23 .A53 2024 (print) | LCC SD421.23 (ebook) | DDC 363.37/9—dc23/eng/20230825

LC record available at https://lccn.loc.gov/2023036389
LC ebook record available at https://lccn.loc.gov/2023036390

ISBN 979-8-3480-2784-1 (pbk.)

Manufactured in the United States of America
4-1012396-49349-4/8/2025

CONTENTS

INTRODUCTION

NO ONE IN THE IDYLLIC TOWN OF PARADISE, CALIFORNIA, could imagine the devastation their small community was about to endure. It started in the early morning hours of November 18, 2018, when a piece of electrical equipment in a canyon of the Sierra Nevada malfunctioned. Then an almost one-hundred-year-old power line fell against a steel tower and melted fragments of metal with its intense heat. As red-hot steel splinters sizzled and rained down on drought-stricken vegetation, a blaze flared up. Unusually strong winds and the dry plants fed the flames, propelling them rapidly, transforming the fire into a raging inferno.

Smoke and ashes darkened Paradise, 7 miles (11 km) from the initial site. In a two-hour span, frightened residents made 132 calls to the Paradise 911 center. Early callers were told that the fire was miles away and that there was no need for concern. A deep canyon lay between the fire and the town. In past instances, the canyon had blocked the advance of wildfires. But the Camp Fire, named for the road on which it started, sped through the canyon, devouring an area

Law enforcement members direct cars out of town during the Camp Fire. Tens of thousands of Paradise residents were evacuated.

equal to eighty American football fields per minute. Shortly after the fire reached Paradise, the county fire department issued a mandatory evacuation of the entire town.

Police officers pounded on doors, calling on residents to leave. "There was just thousands upon thousands of embers blowing through

The Camp Fire gained notoriety as the deadliest and most destructive wildfire in California history. Scientists study the role that droughts and intense heat waves, both exacerbated by climate change, play in fire's increased destructivity.

the air," David Hawks, the California Department of Forestry and Fire Protection (CAL FIRE) unit chief, Butte County, said. "It was really hard to get your mind around how rapidly it was developing. In less than an hour, the fire swept across the town of Paradise, overwhelming the firefighters' efforts to stop it."

Roads became choked as townsfolk attempted to flee. As traffic inched forward, the flames blocked escape routes. With a long line of cars backed up at the intersection of Skyway and Clark in the center of town, firefighters made the only decision they could. They helped people out of their cars and onto an adjacent concrete parking lot. A gun store, a yard full of propane tanks, and a gas station surrounded the lot with highly combustible substances. But the concrete and metal roofs of two nearby buildings under construction might withstand the flames. And because the landscape dipped, forming a low basin, the parking lot was somewhat sheltered from the wind and glowing embers.

People, cats, and dogs huddled helplessly in the parking lot. "Are we gonna die?" many people asked. Though frightened themselves, firefighters did everything they could to reassure their charges. A house across the street burst into flame, and firefighters decided one of the buildings, a coffee shop with a metal roof, would provide better protection. They shattered the large front window and helped people into the building. All they could do was wait and pray. Throughout the city, others hoped and waited in parking lots, in houses, and even in a Walgreens drugstore.

Within four hours, Paradise lay in ruins. Fifty thousand people had been safely evacuated from the town. Residents who had sheltered in the parking lot in the center of town and in the Walgreens store were among those who survived the flames.

Firefighters struggled to contain the fire for over two weeks until rain finally extinguished the blaze. Over 150,000 acres (60,700 ha), a region about the size of Chicago, had been scorched. Eventually, the death toll would reach at least eighty-five, not including those who died indirectly from the disruption of their health care.

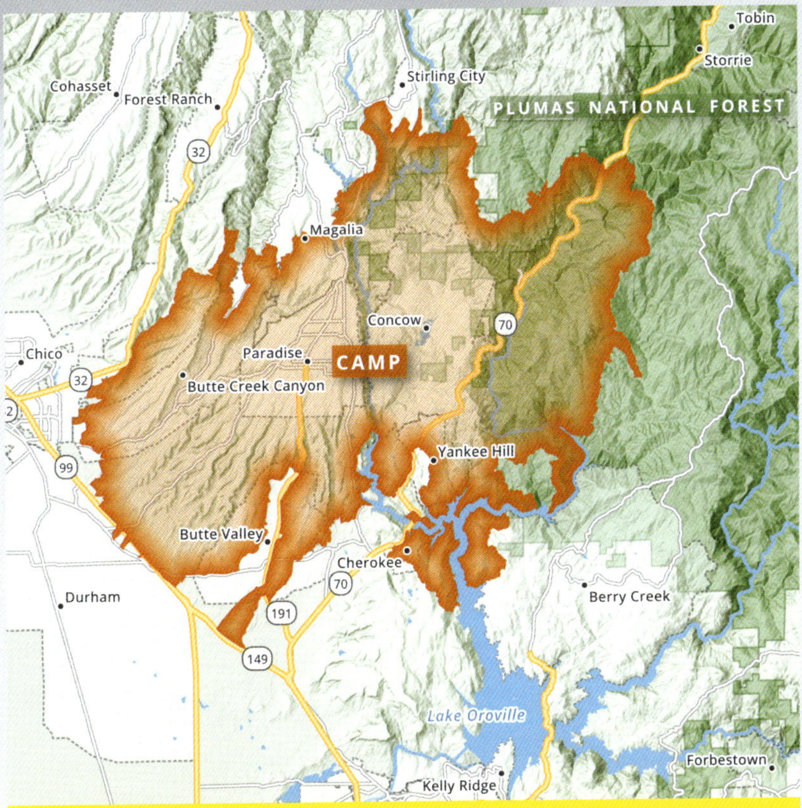

A map of Paradise's 2018 Camp Fire shows how far the wildfire spread before it was put out.

Grasses and other plants can quickly take root after fires, even in heavily burned areas.

Not the Whole Story

The Camp Fire gained notoriety as the deadliest and most destructive wildfire in California history. Unfortunately, fires of such terrifying size seem to be growing in number. Although the annual number of wildfires decreased slightly between the 1990s and the 2020s, the number of acres burned has more than doubled in the same time span. Scientists study the role that droughts and intense heat waves, both exacerbated by climate change, play in fire's increased destructivity. Federal, state, and local firefighters battle walls of flame that seem unstoppable.

But destructive megafires are not the whole story. Naturally occurring fires have always been an indispensable part of nature. Low- and medium-intensity flames eliminate dry and overgrown vegetation from forest floors, reducing the amount of fuel a future fire will encounter. This lessens the chance that a fire will grow out of control. Fire also clears space for new growth, benefiting many plants and animals. Certain species of plants and animals depend on fire for their very survival. Many studies show that even areas severely burned by towering flames rebound quickly with rich biodiversity.

Many studies show that even areas severely burned by towering flames rebound quickly with rich biodiversity.

Many ecologists say that fire is necessary for healthy forests, prairies, and other habitats. But some land managers fear the destructive power of fire and worry that it could spiral out of control to the detriment—rather than benefit—of the environment. Indigenous peoples, who inhabited the Americas millennia before Europeans arrived, provide a third perspective by respecting the power of fire and using their vast understanding of the environment to set cultural burns. These low, carefully managed fires favor species of plants and animals they relied on. In the late 1960s and 1970s, environmentalists began looking to the fire traditions and wisdom of Indigenous peoples for insight about the best way to manage a landscape and promote a flourishing ecology. Should fire that does not threaten human communities be extinguished or allowed to burn itself out naturally?

CHAPTER ONE

Fire Ecology

THE WORLD'S FIRST NATIONAL PARK, YELLOWSTONE, COVERS over 2 million acres (809,400 ha) and boasts a vast assortment of wildlife, over three hundred geysers, more than 290 waterfalls, and thousands of miles of hiking trails. In the summer of 1988, 248 separate fires encompassed this pristine and beloved wilderness. Flames swept through about 1.2 million acres (485,620 ha) in the

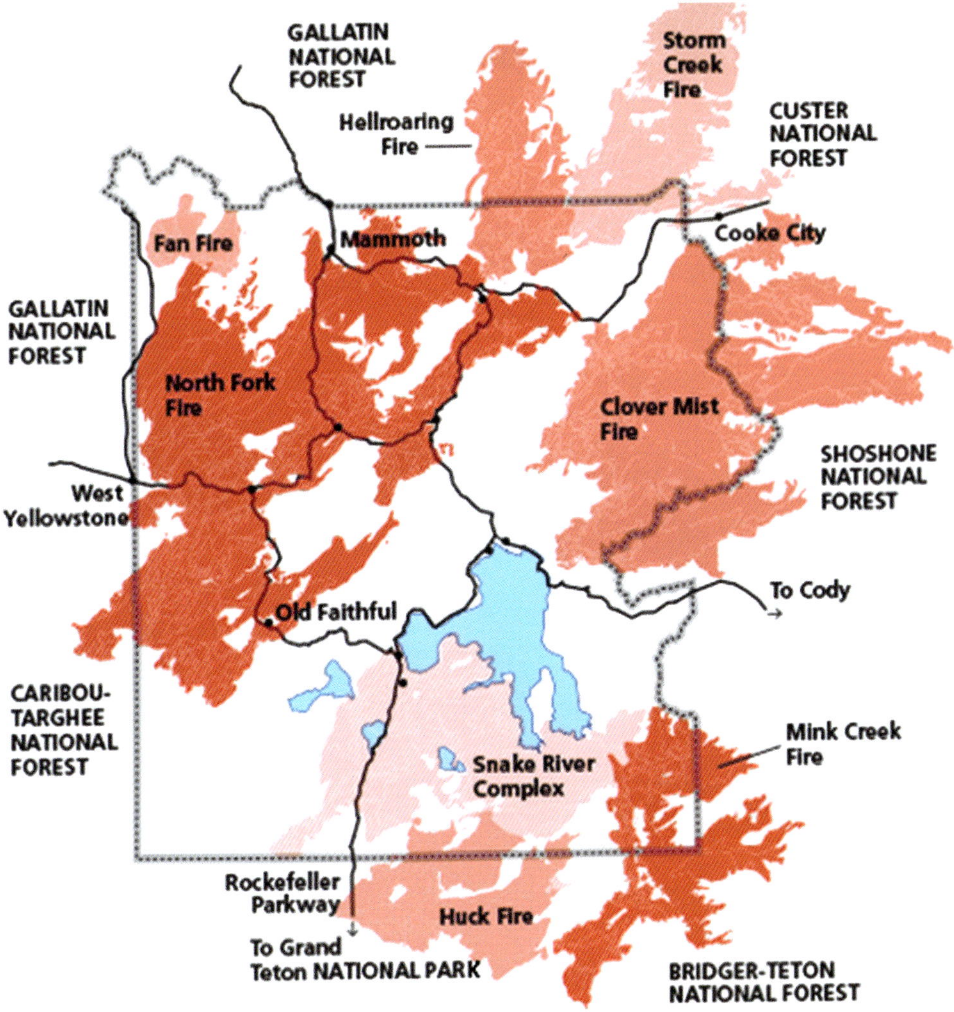

A map of fires from 1988 in Yellowstone. The colors mark the boundaries of separate fires.

park and nearby areas. The sheer magnitude amazed scientists and land managers. Even with twenty-five thousand firefighters and $120 million devoted to extinguishing the conflagration, some of the blazes continued into autumn. Images of a blackened wasteland dominated the air waves. Many media reports painted a scene of devastation, likely to last for decades. A shocked nation believed that it had lost an irreplaceable treasure.

Fires help lodgepole pine cones open to shed new seeds.

But Yellowstone had endured intense fires before. So, it wasn't surprising that by the spring of 1989, wildflowers sprouted in the ash soil. Grasses germinated from roots that survived underground. Over time, more plants began to grow in the sunlight that filtered down into spaces opened up by the fire. By 1998 tiny lodgepole pines had sprung up. Although this species has thin bark and burns easily, many produce thick, strong pine cones with large numbers of seeds. Heat from a fire opens the pine cones and allows the seeds to fall to the ground, where they eventually sprout. Slowly, other species native to the area began to regenerate. Monica Turner, a professor of ecology at the University of Wisconsin, has studied the rejuvenation of Yellowstone since the beginning of her career in 1989. Visiting the scene in 2018, thirty years after the fire, she found flourishing "scenery and wildlife amidst a sea of green." Contrary to the fears of many scientists and wilderness lovers, Yellowstone's ecology was thriving.

The story of Yellowstone's revival is not unique. Many local ecologies in national parks and other areas have rebounded from fire. Even before a specific environment is fully restored, there is much to observe and admire. "A forest in the midst of fire recovery has its own unique beauty that draws people," Josh Durham of the conservation group Trailkeepers of Oregon explained. "The regenerative process in a burn area encourages growth."

Keystone Process

Recovery from a fire depends not only on the survival techniques that certain plants have evolved but also on the nature of the fire itself. Scientists use the phrase *fire regime* to describe the relationship between a specific locale and the kind of fire it is likely to endure on a recurring basis. Factors that determine a fire regime include the frequency of fire in a particular area, the intensity, the extent to which it spreads, and the season in which it occurs.

Fire is one of many factors that make up an ecosystem, a geographic area in which plants, animals, and other organisms interact with one another and the environment. Sunlight, temperature, humidity, atmospheric pressure, wind, rocks, and soil composition work together to form an ecosystem. Every aspect is part of a delicate balance. For example, a change in temperature, an excessive rainfall, or a fire affects the growth of vegetation. This, in turn, affects the animals, which may find that the plants they eat no longer grow in abundance. The entire nature of the ecosystem may change.

Fire is so crucial in maintaining stable ecosystems that it is often considered a *keystone process*—something necessary, even indispensable, for a healthy environment. Without fire to clear away dry twigs and branches, fallen leaves, pine needles, withered vines, and other remains of organic matter, a forest may become choked with debris. By reducing the number of trees, fire allows more sunlight to penetrate the forest canopy, the cluster of overhead foliage. Ashes, rich in nutrients from the burned vegetation, provide fertile ground for new growth, beginning ecological succession as the forest slowly grows back. The exact species of plants to grow back after a fire depend on location, climate, and ecology. The first plants to reappear after a fire of hickory and oak trees are annuals that live only a year. Fast-growing weeds and grasses soon

FIRE SUCCESS STORY: THE BUFF-BREASTED FLYCATCHER

The buff-breasted flycatcher, a species of bird that requires fire to maintain its habitat in ponderosa pine and mixed-conifer (pine cone–bearing) forests, was in trouble at the turn of the century. Decades of aggressive firefighting rendered the forests denser and much harder for the birds to find suitable nesting sites. Over 90 percent of their natural environment in the American Southwest had disappeared. Their numbers declined to reflect a threat of extinction. But after 2000, a series of mixed-intensity wildfires broke out in southeastern Arizona and southwestern New Mexico, burning through forests where the birds had not been seen in many years. The ecological changes from the fire, such as reducing low-lying tangled shrubs without destroying large trees, made the environment well-suited for buff-breasted flycatchers, and they began to appear in large numbers again.

A buff-breasted flycatcher in Arizona in 2014

follow. When these plants become established, taller, slower-growing vegetation such as shrubs begins to appear. The sequence proceeds to small pine trees, bigger pine trees, and finally hardwood trees such as oak and hickory that live for a long time and create a dense canopy. It takes around 150 years to restore a forest.

As the forest evolves through each stage, different plants and animals find food and shelter within its boundaries. When treetops become choked with overgrowth, the canopy blocks light from filtering down. A fire opens the area up again, allowing the cycle to repeat and the forest to rejuvenate. Although forests begin to rebound quickly after a fire, full restoration may take one hundred years or more.

Pyrophytes

Varieties of plants known as pyrophytes (from the Greek words *pyro* for fire and *phyte* for plant) have evolved ingenious ways to protect themselves from fire to ensure the survival of their species. Pyrophytes are classified into two groups: active and passive. Active pyrophytes depend on fire to prevent other species from encroaching on their habitat. So perhaps it is not surprising that they have developed in ways that promote the spread of fire. Eucalyptus trees (or gum trees) are a prime example. Native to Australia and common in California, eucalyptus trees produce a highly flammable oil that vaporizes at high temperatures. Lightning or careless hikers can easily ignite the strips of bark and dead leaves that accumulate around the tree. Quick to catch fire, a eucalyptus tree burns until the surrounding tinder is consumed, and the fire moves on. Most of the trunk is spared, which can then sprout new branches.

Unlike their active counterparts, passive pyrophytes endure fire but do not contribute to its spread. For example, ponderosa pines are covered with a scaly, thick bark that protects the inner layers of their trunks from the fire, thereby allowing water and nutrients to continue moving through the tree. But that's not all. As ponderosa pines age,

Active pyrophytes such as eucalyptus trees can not only endure fire but even benefit from it.

they lose their lower branches, making it harder for fire to rise up the tree and destroy the newer, green needles up high. Other fire-resistant plants, such as some shrubs of the South African species protea, have moist tissues that insulate them and prevent them from drying out during a fire.

Still other plants, labeled pyrophilic, cannot reproduce without fire. Several species of pine trees fall into this group. Because their seeds are sealed with resin in hard cones, they may stay on the tree for years. It takes the heat of a fire to melt the resin, which allows the seeds to fall to the ground and sprout. Plants such as buckbrush and manzanita produce seeds with a tough covering that prevents them from germinating until fire breaks them open. Chemicals in the smoke and in the ash-enriched soil left by the fire may contribute to seedling growth.

Snag Forests

Animals cope with fire in a number of practical ways. Fast runners such as deer flee the encroaching flames. Smaller, less rapid animals such as squirrels, frogs, or rabbits burrow underground or find refuge under a rock or a toppled tree trunk. Others find safety in nearby ponds or streams. When the coast is clear, animals emerge to seek food and shelter in a radically altered world—but one that still has much to offer them.

Snag forests are areas in which fire has destroyed most of the vegetation. Standing dead trees (snags) and thick toppled trunks create a bleak picture, but almost immediately the blackened earth begins to regenerate. Increased sunlight and nutrients in the newly burned soil encourage the growth of flowering shrubs and wildflowers. Many species of insects, such as dragonflies, bees, and flying beetles, are drawn to the new plants. Birds come to nest in the shrubs and feed on the insects. Snowshoe hares, wood rats, and other small mammals find shelter in downed logs and bushes. They become prey for larger animals, such as bears and wolves. Elk and deer find abundant food in the flourishing vegetation. Well-nourished calves and fawns grow quickly.

Just as some plants require fire to flourish, some animals, such as the black-backed woodpecker, depend on fire to sustain them. Unless one looks closely, these birds are difficult to distinguish from the burned tree trunk they are pecking. Months, or sometimes just weeks, after fire has gone through a forest, they arrive to feast on beetles and other insects that bore into the trees' scorched remains. The male woodpecker uses his sharp beak to dig several holes in the charred wood. The female then chooses the hole in which they will make their nest and raise their young. The leftover cavities provide habitats for other animals such as nuthatches, bluebirds, and flying squirrels that are unable to dig their own. Dependent on the black-backed woodpecker for their nesting sites, these other animals

Certain animals, including black-backed woodpeckers, rely on charred forests as habitats.

too have benefited from fire. The habits and needs of many animals are mutually beneficial in the aftermath of a fire.

Fire in the Plains

Fire is also essential to vast, treeless prairies where grasses can grow up to 6 feet (1.8 m) tall. As the grasses age over time, large amounts of decaying matter build up, keeping the soil cold and making it harder for new plants to sprout. Bison, deer, and cattle struggle to find fresh, nourishing grasses to eat. But when a fire reduces the layers of biomass (organic matter such as the decayed grass) to ashes and destroys trees that have begun to take root, the original ecology of the prairie is restored. Nutrients are released into the soil, and sunlight warms the ground again. New grasses flourish, and animals return to graze.

"Fire is what keeps the prairie a prairie," Bill Sproul, a rancher in eastern Kansas, said. "If you take out fire, it changes everything."

DIFFERENT TYPES OF ECOSYSTEMS

Ecosystems are classified into two basic types, aquatic and terrestrial. Both water-based and land-based ecosystems contain biotic (living) elements and abiotic (nonliving) components. The exact number of ecosystems is unknown. According to the *Encyclopedia of Global Warming and Climate Change*, the main types of ecosystems include these:

- ***Temperate forests*** of deciduous, hardwood trees that occupy much of the eastern United States and Europe
- ***Tropical rainforests***, or jungles, of tall trees and densely packed foliage and vines (which allow little sunlight to filter through) that are found in Central and South America
- ***Deserts*** of parched land that receive from 0 to 10 inches (0 to 25 cm) of rainfall per year
- ***Grasslands***, or prairies, consisting of vast areas dominated by almost unbroken stretches of grass and herbs
- ***Taiga***, an occasionally swampy area punctuated by lakes and marshes of coniferous forests (particularly pines, spruce, and larches) in far northern latitudes
- ***Tundra***, a flat, treeless region of the Arctic with layers of permafrost—subsurface soil that remains frozen all year
- ***Chaparral***, a region of shrubs and dwarf trees adapted to dry summers and moist winters, especially found in Southern California
- ***Oceans***, vast bodies of salt water supporting an abundance of plant and animal life

GOPHER TORTOISES

Gopher tortoises, considered a keystone species in the rich forest ecology of sunny longleaf pines, also need fire to maintain a healthy habitat. Like the tunneling rodent for which it is partly named, gopher tortoises dig burrows, sometimes 10 feet (3 m) deep. The burrows keep them safe from predators, extreme heat or cold, and fire. Many other animals also shelter in the spacious holes the tortoises dig.

Periodic wildfire keeps the longleaf pines that gopher tortoises use as homes from being crowded out by invasive species of trees and dense, woody vegetation. Grasses and plants, which are important to the gopher tortoises' diet, grow in the open, sunny spaces created by the fire. Without fire, dark, overgrown forests reduce sunlight, and the tortoises have a hard time regulating their body temperature and finding warm spots in which to burrow. When the gopher tortoise suffers, the whole ecology suffers. But when periodic fires keep the longleaf pine forests open, the gopher tortoise and more than 350 other species can thrive.

A prescribed burn in a longleaf pine forest passes safely over a gopher tortoise den.

Firefighters and environmentalists began to consider using limited prescribed burning to rebuild healthy, resilient ecosystems—a tool Indigenous peoples had known about and practiced all along.

As long ago as the end of the last ice age (about 11,500 years ago), the Indigenous populations of the Great Plains of the American Midwest sophisticatedly used fire to burn withered vegetation. That kept the grasslands open to encourage the return of herds of bison that they hunted for meat, shelter, and cultural materials.

During the 1830s, the US government used treaties to displace Native Americans. Dispossessed of their ancestral lands, the Indigenous peoples of North America were prohibited from practicing their traditional fire practices. The ban resulted in dense, dark forests that were choked with debris and dead vegetation. Trees encroached on prairies, harming native grasses. Dead leaves and dry branches accumulated on the ground. The excess of withered plants fueled naturally occurring fires. Increasingly frequent and severe droughts and heat waves added to the fire danger. Due to all these factors, many experts believe that what once may have been low or moderately intense fires had become larger and more destructive. Firefighters and environmentalists began to consider using limited prescribed burning to rebuild healthy, resilient ecosystems—a tool Indigenous peoples had known about and practiced all along.

CHAPTER TWO

What Is Fire?

FROM THEIR FIRST ENCOUNTERS WITH FIRE, PREHISTORIC PEOPLE were fascinated and frightened. No one knows exactly how humans discovered ways to use fire. Our earliest ancestors may have found it easier to forage for food in the empty spaces fire opened than they did in areas of dense undergrowth. Birds' eggs and small mammals or lizards that had been charred (or "cooked") by fire were likely easier to eat and tasted better than food that had not been burned. Eventually, early humans found ways to tame and keep a small fire so they could cook their own food. "Fire preservers" learned to use slow-burning fuel, such as animal dung, to keep a fire going. Since the people had no way of kindling fire from scratch, the fire was never allowed to go out. Then, sometime between 120,000 and 700,000 years ago, humans around the world learned to start a fire for themselves.

Cooking profoundly changed human development. Cooked food provided more energy and may have led to an increase in the size of the brain. Because cooking took time, humans had to wait to consume their food. Some scientists speculate that waiting prompted an advance

PROMETHEUS STEALS FIRE

Not surprisingly, many early people worshipped fire or believed it came from the gods. In the ancient Greek myth of Prometheus, people suffered in cold darkness because the god Zeus would not share fire with them. Determined to help humanity, Prometheus picked a stalk of fennel, which has a hollow center filled with spongy tissue that would burn slowly. After climbing to the top of Mount Olympus, he stole a spark of lightning and set the fennel on fire. Then he hurried back to the earth and taught humans how to use fire to keep warm and light their way at night. When Zeus realized what had happened, he was furious and had Prometheus chained to a mountain, where he remained for many years until the hero Hercules released him.

in social skills. While sitting around a campfire watching meat or vegetation cook slowly, early people had the chance to gather and talk with one another. Fire and the heat it provided also made the migration from warmer environments to colder northern locales possible.

But fire continued to mystify people. It flickered and moved, almost as if it were alive. It provided light at night, warmth on freezing days, and protection from dangerous animals. But fire also scorched the earth and caused painful injuries, destruction, and death. Lightning sent fire from the sky, and volcanoes brought fire from the depths of the earth. What was this powerful force with both heavenly and earthly origins?

The Fire Triangle

Ancient Greek philosophers thought fire was one of the four basic elements that they believed made up all of nature. But unlike the other substances—earth, air, and water—fire isn't a solid, gas, or liquid. Fire isn't a substance at all. It is a chemical reaction.

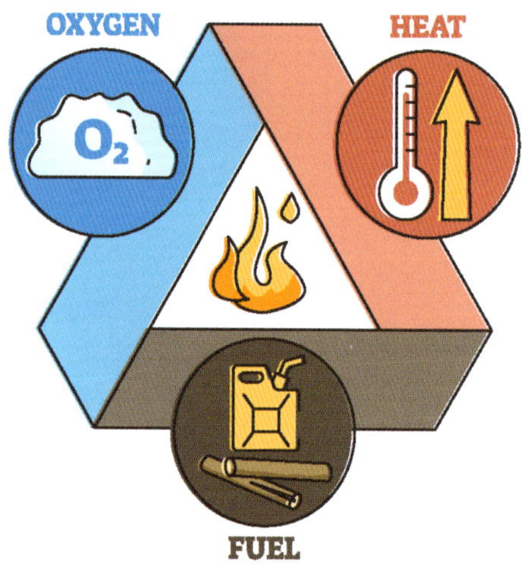

The fire triangle describes the necessary components for creating fire.

Three things are necessary for fire to occur: fuel, heat, and oxygen. They are often called the fire triangle. The fuel consists of combustible materials—that is, substances that catch fire and easily burn such as oil, wood, plants, paper, and fabric. These are called hydrocarbons. They contain both hydrogen and carbon. Metal and stone, which are not hydrocarbons, do not burn under normal circumstances. The heat, a form of energy that may come from a variety of sources such as a match, friction, or lightning, raises the temperature of the fuel to its ignition point. As hydrocarbons heat up, their atoms vibrate faster and faster until they break apart into individual hydrogen and carbon atoms. The carbon combines with oxygen in the air to produce the gas

THE DISCOVERY OF OXYGEN

In the 1700s, many scientists thought that any substance that burned contained a colorless, weightless substance known as phlogiston that released during combustion. But did phlogiston really exist? French chemist Antoine Lavoisier, considered one of the founders of modern chemistry, made an interesting discovery in 1772. When sulfur or phosphorus burned, the ashes weighed more than the original substance. Lavoisier theorized that what had burned had also combined with the air or something in the air—hence the weight gain. The hypothetical phlogiston was not needed to explain fire after all.

Later, Lavoisier learned that English chemist Joseph Priestley had heated mercuric oxide, which released a colorless gas in 1794. The gas could reignite a dying candlewick and even support the breathing of mice. Lavoisier realized this gas must be responsible for why ashes of sulfur or phosphorus weigh more than the original substance. He named the new gas oxygen. Although it comprised a limited amount of the atmosphere, nothing could burn without it.

carbon dioxide (CO_2), and the hydrogen atoms combine with oxygen to form water vapor. The intense heat of these reactions releases energy in the form of photons, or particles of light. Combustion is taking place, and the fuel is burning.

Ignition Temperatures

A great deal of heat is required for a substance to catch fire. Different materials ignite at different temperatures. The amount of heat needed for a particular substance to ignite in the presence of a spark is called the piloted ignition temperature. If the heat is much greater, it may reach the unpiloted ignition temperature, and the substance can catch fire even without a spark. Size and shape also help determine how quickly an object ignites. Something large such as a massive tree will not burn as easily as a twig, sapling, or piles of dry leaves. The fire itself generates enough heat to keep the fuel at its ignition temperature. As long as there is oxygen, heat, and something to burn, the fire will keep going.

Fire generates several natural by-products. Particles of carbon, carbon dioxide, and steam—the result of incomplete combustion—rise as smoke. Only char, ash, and soot are left after fuel burns. Blackened tree trunks in the wake of a wildfire provide a dramatic example of char. Soot, a flaky substance formed by the incomplete combustion of carbon, is scattered by wind and may darken the sky for miles.

Extinguishing a Wildfire

People put fires out in two main ways. When water is thrown on a fire, the intense heat turns the water into steam, or water vapor. In a wildfire, this layer of water vapor keeps the fuel from direct contact with the oxygen it needs to keep burning. The water also lowers the temperature of the dried underbrush and vegetation serving as the fire's fuel. The fire's heat diminishes, and ultimately the flames are extinguished.

Fire retardants, often dropped from airplanes, are also used to battle wildfire. Composed mostly of water and fertilizer, with a few other minor ingredients, fire retardants interfere with the reaction between the flames and the fuel. Water within the vegetation turns to steam, leaving nothing but carbon behind. This reaction lowers the fire's temperature and slows it down. Once a fire has been extinguished, the fertilizer in the retardant may contribute to the environment's regeneration.

NO FIRE ON ANCIENT EARTH

It may be hard to imagine a world without fire, but in the earliest days, when the earth was still a barren rock, fire did not exist. Neither did life. At the time, about 3.5 billion years ago, life began in the ocean. As plants such as kelp, phytoplankton, and algal plankton developed over eons on the surface of the ocean, profound changes began to take place in the earth's atmosphere. Through photosynthesis, the plants converted carbon dioxide and sunlight into sugars they could use and released leftover oxygen into the air. The oxygen level increased from about 13 percent to 17 percent of the atmosphere with the appearance of woody shrubs and trees 360 million years ago, about 100 million years after the first land plants. That increase was enough to allow fire to burn. The wood and vegetation provided plentiful fuel. When lightning struck, ignition took place. The fire triangle of fuel, oxygen, and heat was complete.

COLORS OF FLAME

Although the color red is most often associated with fire, flames can glow in several colors. Temperature plays a major role in what color you see. Between about 980°F and 1,800°F (527°C and 982°C), fires glow red. As the temperature rises to between 2,000°F and 2,200°F (1,093°C and 1,204°C), the flame changes to orange. Between 2,400°F and 2,700°F (1,316°C and 1,482°C), the fire burns white. The hottest fires of all blaze blue at temperatures beginning around 2,600°F to 3,000°F (1,427°C to 1,649°C). For example, burners on gas stoves glow with blue light. Chemicals present in the substance being burned also play a role in determining a flame's color. Hydrocarbons such as oil and natural gas give off a blue light. If a flame burns pink, its fuel probably contains lithium. A green flame indicates the presence of tungsten. One of the best examples of colored flames can be seen in fireworks. The color of the firework depends on the presence of metal salts. For example, strontium produces bursts of red, sodium yellow, barium green, and copper blue.

Because of the chemicals present in the wood, driftwood fires sometimes burn unusual colors such as blue, green, or pink.

Water is one of the most basic and common substances used to put out fires.

Fire as a Tool

Fire itself also stimulates regrowth after purging an area of dense underbrush and dried-out vegetation. The blaze creates ash rich in nutrients that growing seedlings need. It creates opens spaces, allowing sunlight to reach the forest floor. A burned environment allows species such as the gopher tortoise and black-backed woodpecker to thrive. Fire traditions also created favorable conditions for grazing animals that were hunted for food and hides.

Understanding such processes is vital to maintaining healthy ecosystems that support human welfare. Knowing how fire promotes regrowth can be carefully applied to achieve specific goals such as growing a particularly useful plant for food or medicine. When a fire is purposefully set to benefit a population's well-being and livelihood, it becomes a valuable tool—one used by Indigenous peoples all over the world.

CHAPTER THREE

Land Needs Fire: Indigenous Fire Practices

FOR MILLENNIA, INDIGENOUS PEOPLES ACROSS THE GLOBE HAVE understood the requirements of fire, as well as its behavior. Fire is an essential part of nature, a tool to help them manage the land, and a gift from the Creator. By burning layers of dead vegetation that could otherwise become fuel, carefully tended fires lessened the chance of a disastrous wildfire. But Indigenous fire use is about much

Crews work on Yurok land in California to burn undergrowth on the forest floor. Cultural burns help wildlife, promote new growth, and more.

more than clearing the land of potentially flammable debris. Closely tied to livelihood, traditions, beliefs, values, and spirituality, fire is a way of life for many Indigenous peoples. Children learn to respect fire and to use it with the greatest care. They grow up with a sense of responsibility to the land that supports them and to the wildlife that benefits from their thoughtful, judicious use of fire.

"Fire itself is sacred," Bill Tripp, director for the Karuk Tribe Department of Natural Resources, wrote. "It renews life. It shades rivers and cools the water's temperature. It clears brush and makes for

HOW GRANDMOTHER SPIDER GAVE PEOPLE FIRE

The Indigenous peoples of North America have long shared stories about a fire-bringer. In the Choctaw version of this story found on the Mississippi Band of Choctaw's website, the people and animals were encased in cold and wretched darkness. When they learned that people to the east had fire to give them warmth and light, they decided to send someone to steal it. Opossum tried first, but the fire burned his tail. He was discovered by the eastern people who took away the fire and sent him home. Next, Buzzard tried, but the fire burned his head feathers. Once again, the people of the east retrieved the fire and sent him away. When Crow fared no better, the people's council didn't know who could succeed. "I can!" said Grandmother Spider as loudly as she could. So, Grandmother Spider made a small clay container with a little hole in the lid for air. She spun a web to the east and followed it to the fire. She seized some embers, closed them in the pot, and returned without being caught because she was too tiny to be seen. On arriving home, she lifted the lid, and the fire flared up. But who would take the long-desired flames? The animals, as well as the insects, were afraid of being burned. Only the humans, whom the animals all thought very timid, agreed to take the fire if Grandmother Spider would help them. Grandmother Spider taught the humans how to tend fire, use it for their betterment, and keep themselves safe. For this reason, you often see spiders used in Choctaw art and displayed in homes.

sufficient food for large animals. It changes the molecular structure of food and fiber resources making them nutrient dense and more pliable. Fire does so much more than western science currently understands."

Indigenous fire practices, known as cultural burns, have been used for generations, an acknowledgment that fire is a sacred gift. Natural sources for ignition are regularly used, but contemporarily, drip torches, metal cans with a wick that trickles flammable liquid to the ground, are also used to start the fire. Crew members walk beside the flames, extinguishing stray embers to ensure the fire stays on course. As they steer the flames across the landscape, they create mosaics of burned and unburned patches.

The fire flickers slowly across the ground, giving animals time to escape. Although the fire burns underbrush, it does not rise high enough to damage the treetop foliage, habitat to many birds and small animals. It enriches the soil and creates favorable conditions for the growth of native plants, which can be used for food and medicine. By burning invasive plants that take up lots of water, the fire allows more water to accumulate in the ground and eventually drain into creeks or rivers. Charcoal that remains on the ground serves as a water purifier, so the water that seeps into streams or rivers after a fire is especially clean.

Shaping the Land

Many landscapes that are taken for granted as simply part of nature have been greatly influenced by the well-considered land management practices of Indigenous peoples long before Europeans arrived in North America. Frank Lake, an Indigenous Forest Service research ecologist, explained: "Indigenous people had been managing those lands for a long time. They are actually cultural fire regimes because [fire practitioners] didn't just live in harmony with fire, they learned to utilize it to create habitat for gain and support sustainable, healthy forests using cultural burns."

Fire has many benefits. For example, research suggests that cultural burns contributed significantly to the abundance of oak and chestnut trees in Appalachia. After the burning, plants would

A GRANDMOTHER'S MISSION

Margo Robbins wanted only the best for her grandchildren. For a member of the Yurok Tribe of Northern California, this meant they should be carried in traditional baby baskets made of hazel. But there was no usable hazel for her to craft the elaborate baskets. All the hazel bushes were jumbled and twisted. Robbins needed stems that were long, straight, and pliable. The only way hazel grew such stems was after fire purged the plants.

For many years, there had been no cultural burns in the Yurok community. Then, in 2013, Yurok members partnered with CAL FIRE to conduct a 7-acre (2.8 ha) burn on their ancestral lands. It was a deeply meaningful and joyful occasion for the Yurok. After the fire, the hazel grew straight and long again. At last, Robbins could weave baskets for her grandbabies. Determined to promote more cultural burning, Robbins also became an executive director of the community-based Cultural Fire Management Council.

Robbins shows a baby basket made of hazel.

rebound with renewed vitality. The sugar pine forests of the Sierra Nevada also benefited from Indigenous fires that reduced competition from invasive species. And tallgrass prairies in the American Midwest were burned at regular intervals to stimulate new growth that would lure bison.

Fire has benefited people too. "As aboriginal people, we feel like if you take care of country, country will take care of you," Shawn Colbung, a member of the Noongar people of Australia, explained. That philosophy has proved valid for Indigenous peoples across the globe who use fire in many creative and practical ways. Fire can clear a pathway for travel through dense vegetation and forests. It can drive prey into open hunting grounds, create firebreaks around communities, and decrease the number of stinging insects or pests that harm plants that people wish to grow. For example, when fire destroys acorn weevils in oak trees, people and animals receive a more plentiful harvest of acorns. And fire can shape the way hazel plants grow so that people can use their tall, pliant branches as weaving sticks to make baby baskets, eel traps, eating bowls, and much more.

Australia: Fire Helps the Land

The First Nations peoples of Australia also used fire to create healthy, sustainable habitats. But, like Indigenous peoples in North America, they endured a long interruption of their land management techniques. After World War II (1939–1945), towns, cattle stations, and missions lured First Nations peoples from their homes with promises of jobs and schooling. Missions were created by religious groups to convert First Nations peoples to Christianity and provided housing and training for low-level jobs. Stations were generally administered by government officials. These managers decided who could live on the station and maintained strict control over the lives of the inhabitants. Not only did this distance them from their lands and cultures, but it also took a severe toll on the environment.

Terrah Guymala of the Bininj Nation became aware of the crisis when he was a child living at a mission station in the 1970s. Seeing smoke billow on the horizon, he learned that wildfires were ravaging his people's ancestral territories in Arnhem Land in northeastern Australia. Concerned elders knew the countryside needed their care again and decided to return. Guymala and his family became part of the homelands movement, led by world-famous First Nations artist Bardayal "Lofty" Nadjamerrek in the 1970s. Families and small, closely related groups left the missions and settlements where life became increasingly unstable both politically and socially. Leaders of the homelands movement hoped that a return to ancestral lands would benefit communities.

In the absence of First Nations caretakers and the small-scale fires they had carefully set, the ecology of the savanna, rainforests, and floodplains in the region had changed drastically. Feral cats and buffalo, previously unknown in the area, had taken up residence, while animals that had once occupied the locale, such as emus, were growing scarce. Non-native weeds flourished, but centuries-old anbinik trees—an important source of wood and antiseptic made from the sap—were in serious trouble. Biodiversity had declined, and trees had sprouted in regions that were previously grasslands. Guymala, now a senior ranger with the Warddeken Land Management, summarized the situation: "Land needs fire."

"Land needs fire."

Since the start of the West Arnhem Land Fire Abatement project in 1997, First Nations and non-First Nations Australians have come together to create fire management programs that combine cultural burning wisdom and modern scientific technology. Their goal is to lessen the danger from wildfire, reduce carbon emissions, increase biodiversity, and give the people who returned to their Native lands a chance to use their ancestors' knowledge and provide for their families.

BARDAYAL "LOFTY" NADJAMERREK

Nadjamerrek (*second from left*) sits in front of some of his artwork with (*left to right*) his grandson Maath Maralngurra, granddaughter Lorraine White, and daughter June Nadjamerrek in 2006. Nadjamerrek was esteemed for his art and his impact on the homelands movement.

Born around 1926 in Australia's West Arnhem Land, Bardayal "Lofty" Nadjamerrek grew up watching his father and other artists carry on an ancient tradition by painting images on the rock walls and canyons of the starkly beautiful "stone country." He created his first rock art as a young teenager and began his professional career as a painter in 1969. In addition to commanding national respect as an artist, Nadjamerrek was widely esteemed for helping First Nations families reclaim their homelands through the homelands movement. He became deeply involved in establishing six outstations, small communities on First Nations land that had special cultural or economic significance to the families, either culturally or economically. The community he founded through these outstations became an educational center for topics such as art history, botany, ecology, anthropology, linguistics, and First Nations land management. In 2004 he was made an Officer of the Order of Australia "for service to the preservation of Indigenous culture as a Senior Traditional man and significant artist whose work documents the relationship of the land and its ancestral past via the Mimih Spirits of rock art."

Africa and the Amazon: Each Fire Different

Guymala's observation applies well beyond Australia's borders. The landscapes and ecosystems of Africa and South America differ greatly from each other. But on each continent, First Nations peoples have

A controlled burn moves through grasslands in Kenya, West Africa. Prescribed burns can help clear and rejuvenate many kinds of ecosystems.

studied the environment carefully, made profound connections with nature, and found ways to make fire work for themselves and for the well-being of many species. Before Europeans colonized Africa, African farmers ignited and tended small fires in grasslands and wooded areas. Each fire was different, the result of carefully studying the environment to preserve necessary plants and protect wildlife. Purging the land of withered vegetation allowed new grasses to sprout and kept the land open for grazing animals. Frequent fires, both human-made and natural, caused trees to develop thick, fire-resistant bark. Careful monitoring of cultural burns ensured that 95 percent of the trees survived the fires.

In South America, Natives of the Amazon rainforests have traditionally used fire to maintain the small plots—generally 1.2 acres (0.5 ha)—in which they grow crops. After several years, the farmers move on to other areas, giving the land time to regenerate. As in other locales, the patchlike pattern of burned and unburned ground keeps dried-out vegetation at a minimum and creates natural firebreaks, which both reduce the chances of a natural fire spiraling out of control.

Depending on the topography, the physical features of a landscape, fire can be used in many resourceful and sustainable ways. In a remote region of the Brazilian Amazon, the Mebengokre (Kayapo) people burn the tall savanna grasses, making it easier to hunt burrow-dwelling tortoises. In the nearby country of Guyana, Wapishana and Macushi peoples use fire to smoke out bees before they gather honey. Throughout the Amazon rainforests, fire promotes a bountiful harvest of certain fruit trees and creates a protective space around homes, farms, and sacred forests.

For Indigenous peoples of the rainforest and of environments across the globe, fire not only sustains them physically, but it is also part of their cultural heritage and ethnic identity. Fire is a legacy too precious to lose.

CHAPTER FOUR

A History of Fire Suppression

AMERICAN HOMESTEADERS HEADING WESTWARD DURING THE California gold rush of 1849 encountered a flourishing landscape of forests and grasslands. An abundance of bison roamed the prairies. A vast variety of animals filled the woodlands. For many pioneers, unaware of the role Indigenous peoples played in managing the land, such abundance could only mean "divine

Wildfires such as the Chicago Fire in 1871 contributed to the public's concern about and fear of fire in the late nineteenth and early twentieth centuries.

intervention." More observant pioneers took note of the carefully tended burns that tribal nations regularly administered to the land. Some newspapers and journals remarked on the practice favorably, while others opposed the Indigenous use of fire as a primitive and dangerous procedure.

A series of frightening wildfires in the second half of the nineteenth century motivated those who considered all fire a threat to life and property. On October 8, 1871, a fire broke out in Chicago and raced through the city, destroying more than seventeen thousand buildings. The fire raged for over twenty-four hours before rain extinguished it. Three hundred people died, and ninety thousand people lost their homes.

Fires that had ignited in the Midwest around the same time were aggravated by hot, dry weather. Although not as well known as the

Chicago Fire, the conflagration in and around Peshtigo, Wisconsin, became "the deadliest fire in American history." High winds drove smaller blazes into fires that raged for two weeks before a shift in the wind propelled the flames toward Peshtigo. The gales flung all sorts of debris, including chunks from buildings into the smoke-filled air. In panic, many people ran for the Peshtigo River, where some drowned. Others were able to wait out the fire in the water. By the time the fire was extinguished, over 1 million acres (404,690 ha) burned, destroying thousands of buildings and sixteen towns. Over fifteen hundred people died.

Protecting the Nation's Forests

The public's memory of devastating fire still lingered when Theodore Roosevelt became president in 1901. An ardent conservationist, Roosevelt established the US Forest Service in 1905 to safeguard the country's forests. Charged with protecting the fresh water and timber in the nation's woodlands, forest rangers would extinguish wildfires and guard against anyone who would illegally exploit the forest for personal gain.

Some people doubted that a government agency was needed to protect America's forests. Gifford Pinchot, the first chief of the burgeoning organization and a personal friend of Roosevelt, was determined to prove the worth of the nation's newest federal agency. But although he spoke about the importance of the forests' natural resources across the country, his efforts did little to convince Americans. After taking office, President William Howard Taft fired Pinchot and Congress stopped the Forest Service's funding in 1910.

The day after his removal, Pinchot tried to boost the spirits of his demoralized staff in Washington. "You are engaged in a piece of work that lies at the foundation of the new patriotism of conservation . . . don't let the spirit of the service decline one-half inch [1.3 cm] . . . stay in the service, stick to the work," he urged. Deafening applause followed his impromptu speech.

HERBERT STODDARD: ADVOCATE OF PRESCRIBED BURNING

Born in 1889, Herbert Stoddard spent part of his childhood in central Florida where his family grew oranges. Unlike most people in the rest of the country, residents of Florida had a profound respect for fire and its benefits. "Everyone lived with and expected fire," said Chris Kinslow, a land manager with St. Johns River Water Management District in Florida. "People swept their yards to keep dried leaves and fuel away from their houses."

Young Stoddard acquired a positive understanding of fire too. He was observant and deeply loved nature. Watching local cattle ranchers set fires in the woods, he learned the importance of carefully controlled burns to the ecology of longleaf pine forests.

As an adult, Stoddard returned to the Red Hills between Georgia and Florida to investigate why the population of bobwhite quails was decreasing. His careful research led him to conclude that a lack of fire was causing the decline. The grasses and plants that flourish after a fire provide a natural habitat for the bobwhite quail. In the absence of fire, woody shrubs that are not suited to the quails' habitat requirements take over. Stoddard's findings led to more prescribed burnings. He continued to advocate for prescribed fire throughout his career.

The Big Blowup

Six months after Pinchot's rousing words, hundreds of small fires broke out in the drought-stricken Rocky Mountains of Idaho and Montana. On August 20, high-velocity winds gusted into the area, fanning the flames into a raging conflagration—the Big Blowup of 1910. "The whole world seemed to us men back in those mountains to be aflame," forest ranger Ed Pulaski would later recall. "Many thought that it really was the end of the world." More than eighty-five people, including seventy-eight firefighters, died as the fire devoured more than 3 million acres (1.2 million ha) in two days and destroyed entire villages. The smoke could be seen as far as New England. Ashes blew across the Atlantic Ocean to Greenland.

Renewed Fire Suppression

The magnitude of the devastation shocked the nation. Once again, Pinchot championed the Forest Service, claiming that with sufficient money and personnel, it could have prevented much of the disaster. This time, Congress listened and doubled its previous funding of the organization. Private citizens listened too. Firefighters who lost their lives were mourned and honored as heroes. People who had been tolerating small fires in environments such as piney woods in the South or sugar pines in the Sierra Nevada began to rethink their views. No one could tell when a fire would rage out of control, threatening communities and reducing thousands of acres or more to blackened ruins. Fire had to be suppressed at all costs. Ever vigilant, always on the front line, the Forest Service would lead the way.

Twenty-five years after the Big Blowup, the 10 a.m. policy underscored the Fire Service's mission. According to this strict firefighting strategy, all fires, even those hundreds of miles from human habitations, had to be under control by 10 a.m. the day after they were discovered. To further its goal, the Forest Service stationed firefighting crews on public lands during the fire season. More than eight thousand lookout towers were built to scan for distant flames. On July 12, 1940, a new era in firefighting began when two smoke jumpers parachuted from a plane into a fire burning in a remote portion of the Nez Perce National Forest in Idaho. Reaching a site by plane instead of by foot gave the men a crucial edge in suppressing the blaze. By the next morning, they had stopped the spread.

ED PULASKI: HERO OF THE BIG BLOWUP OF 1910

For several months, forest ranger Ed Pulaski and his crew had been fighting wildfires in the Bitterroot Mountains of Montana and Idaho. Twenty-five hundred fires had erupted by the second week in August 1910. But soaring temperatures and the harsh terrain drove many quickly recruited firefighters from the job. Then prisoners in Montana were released to fill the ranks. Soon after, President Taft dispatched four thousand troops, including the buffalo soldiers, the first Black men to serve as soldiers in time of peace, to help fight the fires too. For a while, the fires seemed to be almost contained.

Pulaski's crew of exhausted men needed supplies when he left them to get provisions in the nearby town of Wallace, Idaho. As he was returning, sudden winds of 70 miles (113 km) per hour whipped the numerous smaller fires, some almost contained, into a single enormous conflagration. Pulaski found his crew in desperate straits. Towering flames approached. Tall trees toppled. Thick smoke choked them and obscured their vision. "Come on! Come on! Follow me." Guiding his men through the fire, Pulaski led them to a tunnel in an

The Leopold Report

Fire suppression remained the country's official policy for many years. Although increasing numbers of ecologists and foresters believed that fire was important to the well-being of the wilderness, policymakers didn't take note until the 1960s. It began with an overabundance of elk in Yellowstone. Because the park could not support the growing

abandoned mine. The heat was overwhelming. A few men wanted to leave, but Pulaski forced them to remain at gunpoint. His fierce determination saved the lives of most of his men. After the fire passed by, they stumbled down the mountain to Wallace.

Still suffering from damage to his eyes and lungs from the fire, Pulaski continued with the Forest Service until 1929. He also developed a firefighting tool, based on earlier models, with an axe on one end and a hoe on the other. His version was easy to handle and effective. Firefighters all over the world would receive and use the famous tool known as the Pulaski.

The unique construction of the Pulaski allows people to dig small holes with one side and cut vegetation and other materials with the other.

Firefighters douse a fire in water to put it out in the 1920s. Many people believed suppression, such as with water, was the best—and even only—way to approach fire for decades.

numbers, rangers shot 4,283 elk in the winter of 1961–1962. The public uproar over what was perceived as cruelty to these majestic animals prompted Secretary of the Interior Stewart Udall to create a committee to study wildlife management. Aldo Starker Leopold, chair of the committee, a professor at the University of California, Berkeley, and the son of renowned conservationist Aldo Leopold, wrote a paper about the future of national parks in 1963. Nicknamed the Leopold Report, it included recommendations that would profoundly change how the parks were managed. Their purpose, he said, was to "represent a vignette of primitive America" making certain that "the biotic associations within each park be maintained, or where necessary recreated, as nearly as possible in the condition that prevailed when the area was first visited by the white man." In other words, the relationship between the many species of plants and animals should not be changed by human interference. Everything should be preserved in a state of pure nature.

The problem was that non-Indigenous people had interfered already. Fire suppression had changed wilderness ecology in ways that did not surprise the Indigenous peoples separated from their ancestral lands. Leopold included several examples of environmental changes, including the western slope of the Sierra Nevada. He described the land as it would have appeared in 1849 to prospectors on their way to California to join the gold rush. The sturdy, widely spaced trees had allowed plenty of sunlight to reach the forest floor. Leopold called the same area in 1963 "depressing." The previously open forest had been replaced by a "dog-hair thicket of young pines, white fir, incense cedar, and mature brush—a direct function of overprotection from natural ground fires." The way to restore environments to their pristine condition was to reintroduce fire. This meant not only allowing some natural fires to burn unchecked, but it also called for controlled burning.

Not everyone could accept the blunt conclusions of the Leopold Report. Some staff members of the National Park Service sought ways to thwart the reintroduction of fire into America's wilderness. A high-ranking staff member of the National Park Service reacted with indignation to a plan that would allow natural fires to burn unchecked in the Sequoia and Kings Canyon National Parks. "Over my dead body!" he exclaimed.

Little changed until the summer of 1967 when fourteen fires burned out of control in Glacier National Park in Kalispell, Montana. Elsewhere in the state, fires consumed 800 acres (324 ha). Proponents of the Leopold Report used the fires and the growing public concern to affect changes. In 1968 the National Park Service adopted a new policy that recognized "the presence or absence of natural fire within a given habitat . . . as one of the ecological factors contributing to the perpetuation of plants and animals native to that habitat." It also said, "Prescribed burning to achieve approved vegetation and/or wildlife management objectives may be employed as a substitute for natural fire."

SMOKEY BEAR AND REDDY SQUIRREL

Smokey the Bear, the popular mascot of the US Forest Service, dates back to World War II. The public was shocked when enemy submarines off the coast of California fired exploding shells onto an oil field in 1942. Fears grew that more such attacks could spark fires. In the 1940s, few women were firefighters. With most experienced firefighters and other able-bodied men away at war, who would extinguish those fires? To protect the landscape, the Forest Service launched a program encouraging people to be careful. They invented slogans including "Forest Fires Aid the Enemy" and "Our Carelessness, Their Secret Weapon."

On August 9, 1944, Smokey Bear officially became an emblem for the campaign. Artist Albert Staehle completed a poster of a bear emptying a bucket of water over a campfire, the first of many illustrations of Smokey. In 1947 he got a new slogan, "Only you can prevent forest fires," which would become familiar nationwide.

Then, in 1950, firefighters discovered a badly burned bear cub in the Capitan Mountains of New Mexico. The small bear had managed to survive a forest fire by climbing a tree. Sensitive to the bear's injuries and impressed by his courage, the firefighters named him Smokey. Taken to the National Zoo in Washington, DC, this real-life Smokey soon became as well-known as his fictional counterpart. Both helped publicize the message that preventing fires was important.

But Smokey has since become a bit controversial. As people began to understand fire is inevitable and necessary, some questioned the relevance of Smokey's message. His slogan was changed in 2001 to read, "Only you can prevent *wildfires*." Babete Anderson, a representative for the Forest Service, explained the difference between the old and new slogans, saying, "There is good fire and bad fire, that's what his message is."

Smokey Bear continues to be a well-known symbol of wildfire prevention.

To emphasize the point, the Forest Service Employees for Environmental Ethics, an environmental advocacy group, introduced a new mascot in 2002—Reddy Squirrel. Perky in hiking shoes and hard hat and shouldering a rake, Reddy cautions, "No one can prevent forest fires. Be ready."

Mark Blaine, editor of *Forest Magazine* and creator of Reddy Squirrel, did not propose to replace Smokey Bear. "But Reddy has a new message for a new generation," he explained in 2004. "She's a fire mascot who understands fire ecology."

Returning Fire to National Parks

The new policy of prescribed burns began in 1968 in the Sequoia and Kings National Parks. The giant sequoia trees of California's Sierra Nevada can tower up to 250 or 300 feet (76 or 91 m) with trunks near the ground of over 30 feet (9 m) in diameter and 90 feet (27 m) in circumference. But the majestic trees (which can live to be two thousand to three thousand years old) were in trouble. No new trees were growing. The Forest Service issued a study in 1994 titled "Long-Term Dynamics of Giant Sequoia Populations: Implications for Managing a Pioneer Species." The study concluded that sequoias need fire to melt the resin sealing their cones to release their seeds, and that young saplings grow best in the ashes of a recent fire. But fire had other important benefits on the giant sequoia-mixed conifer forest. It recycles nutrients into the soil; prevents the overgrowth of competitive species; helps many species of wildlife; develops a patchwork of different kinds of plants; purges the forest of layers of dead, flammable vegetation; and can lessen the severity of destructive insects and diseases.

In the summer of 1968, qualified park rangers ignited a controlled fire in Sequoia and Kings Canyon National Parks that burned 800 acres (324 ha). Another fire caused by lightning on nearby Rattlesnake Ridge was allowed to burn itself out. The next year, park officials designated almost 15 percent of the park, or 130,000 acres (52,609 ha), where lightning-induced fires would be allowed to burn. Over 6,000 additional acres (2,430 ha) were treated with prescribed burning. Current park rangers still practice prescribed burning, which has continued into the twenty-first century. The hope is to protect young sequoias from disease, drought, damaging insects such as bark beetles, and high-intensity wildfires so they can grow to become giants in the Sierra Nevada parks.

As park rangers in the National Park Service, Forest Service, and other organizations realized the advantages of prescribed burns, they began to appreciate the traditional ecological knowledge of the

Giant sequoias are only one of several types of trees that need fire to grow new saplings.

Indigenous peoples. Eventually, this led to some important partnerships between tribal nations and state and federal organizations. Stewarding the environment goes hand in hand with honoring the culture and sacred traditions of Indigenous peoples. For example, Coast Miwok people—members of the Federated Indians of Graton Rancheria—work closely with the park staff of California's Muir Woods in research, education, revitalization of their cultural traditions, and maintenance of sites that hold special meaning for them.

PHILMONT SCOUT RANCH

In April 2022, Philmont Scout Ranch, a Boy Scout base near Cimarron, New Mexico, was forced to evacuate as the Cooks Peak Fire, driven by winds of 75 miles (121 km) per hour, crossed its border. By the time the fire was contained, at least 3,084 acres (1,248 ha) of the about 220-square-mile (570 sq. km) ranch had burned. Although a cabin and miles of fencing were destroyed, the fire had little impact on Philmont's activities.

Four years earlier, in 2018, wildfire had damaged 27,000 acres (10,930 ha) of the ranch. The staff had taken immediate safety precautions to protect the ranch against future fires. They thinned ponderosa pine forests by removing smaller trees that could act as a ladder to the tall canopy. They also gathered withered debris, possible fuel for a wildfire, and burned them carefully in piles during the winter. "The beauty of it all," Lee Hughes, Philmont's conservation director, said, "is that Scouts from all over the country learn about fire ecology and mitigation work here that they can take back home and begin the process there as well."

Dry, easy-to-burn materials such as dead wood often accumulate around logging roads.

Logging

Despite the gradual acceptance of low-intensity prescribed burns, land managers tended to view high-intensity fires as catastrophes. In 2004 the US Forest Service published a brochure, "Forests with a Future," that drew a sharp distinction between good fires and bad fires. Towering flames that rose to the forest canopy and destroyed many trees were labeled "eco-disaster[s]." To diminish fuel loads and reduce the risk of high-intensity fire, the brochure proposed that national forests be thinned. Loggers would chop down trees, creating open spaces that would not feed a fire.

Land management agencies accepted the idea and initiated extensive logging programs that brought them a great deal of money. They used the income to improve their programs and purchase equipment. But their newfound prosperity took a toll on the environment. Thousands of live and dead trees were cut and sold to logging companies. Since the bigger trees are most profitable to the companies, they are felled most often. Flammable grasses and shrubs fill in the newly opened space between trees, creating more fuel for a possible fire. That space also allows moisture to evaporate from soil and from plants faster and makes it easier for strong winds to blow through the forest rapidly. Rubble from the logging, called slash, further adds to the fuel load. Moreover, logging requires new roads into the forest to haul the lumber, providing an easy entrance for campers and explorers. This causes risks because more fires are started by humans than by natural causes such as lightning. Campfires, sparks from car exhausts, and the use of firearms are some prime causes of fires.

Many people still believe that logging reduces the risk of severe fires. But logging does nothing to remove the withered, flammable biomass accumulated throughout a century of fire suppression. It cannot replace prescribed and cultural burns for restoring forest habitats and lessening the severity of future fires.

CHAPTER FIVE

Climate Change

SMOG OBSCURED THE USUALLY IMPRESSIVE HEADQUARTERS OF the United Nations in New York City. It was June 2023. Wildfires burning out of control hundreds of miles away in Canada blanketed much of the United States with a dense orange haze. Some observers invested the eerie sight of the UN building with symbolism. The smog seemed an ominous reminder

Smoke from the 2023 Canada wildfires was especially dense in parts of the midwestern and northeastern US, such as in New York City, that summer, making it hard to see and breathe outside.

that climate change threatens everyone and that all nations, especially wealthy, industrial nations, have a role to play in mitigating its effects.

Hotter, more intense wildfires are an especially frightening consequence of human-induced climate change. Although several factors contribute to the growing wildfire crisis, scientists view climate change as a prime cause. While not actually causing any individual fire, climate change creates the circumstances that better allow wildfires to spread out of control. In the 1990s, US wildfires burned an average of 3.3 million acres (1.3 million ha) each year. Although fewer overall fires have occurred in the 2000s, more than 7 million acres (2.8 million ha) have burned annually, more than twice that of the 1990s. "Climate change is creating the perfect conditions for larger, more intense wildfires," Robert Scheller, a forestry and environmental resources professor at North Carolina State University, said in 2022. "We're already seeing fires that we didn't expect to see until 2080."

DISASTER ON MAUI

Sometimes a fire moves so quickly that those in its path have little or no warning. That was the case August 9, 2023, on the Hawaiian Island of Maui. Whipped by high winds from Hurricane Dora, a massive storm hundreds of miles distant, the worst of three fires ravaged the historic town of Lahaina, the former royal capital of Hawaii. Some people could only escape the flames by plunging into the ocean, where many were later rescued by the Coast Guard. Twenty-two hundred buildings, mostly homes, were destroyed. When President Biden visited Maui on August 21, the death toll had risen to ninety-nine, surpassing that of the Paradise, California, Camp Fire in 2018. The Lahaina fire became the deadliest fire in the US in one hundred years. Rebuilding would take years and cost billions of dollars.

It is believed that downed power lines sparked the initial blaze on Maui. Higher temperatures and stronger hurricanes in recent years contributed to the fire's severity. An abundance of non-native vegetation that burns easily was another significant factor. "The massive winds, dry winds, are what drove this fire," Josh Stanbro, former chief resilience officer in Honolulu, added. "This is part of a long-term trend that is directly related to climate changes and impacts on the islands."

An especially beloved landmark in Lahaina was the famous 150-year-old banyan tree with multiple vertical roots descending from its branches, forty-six sturdy trunks, and a canopy that stretched over 0.5 acres (0.2 ha). Imported from India in 1873, the 60-foot-high (18 m) tree served as a gathering place for picnics, luaus, memorials to war heroes, and many other activities. While banyans are generally resilient, their thin bark makes them especially susceptible to fire. Blackened and charred, its lush canopy destroyed, Lahaina's banyan remained upright. If its roots escaped damage, tree experts believed it might regenerate, and new sprouts in the canopy in late September signaled possible recovery. President Biden called the banyan tree "a very powerful symbol of what we can and will do to get through this crisis."

Fires across the World

As heat waves and droughts have become more common over the last several decades, traditional fire seasons have lengthened in Australia, the western United States, and other parts of the globe. Between June 2019 and October 2020, wildfires in Australia scorched more than 59 million acres (23.9 million ha) of bushlands, a disaster known as the country's Black Summer. The fire directly resulted in the death of 33 people. Almost 450 more later died from the effects of smoke inhalation.

California has also experienced an increase in wildfire casualties and in the amount of land burned. According to a study published by the National Academy of Sciences in 2023, the area blackened by wildfires in California increased by 172 percent between 1971 and 2021. In 2020 alone, almost 4.4 million acres (1.8 million ha) burned.

TWO KINDS OF FIRE

The United Nations Environment Programme draws a distinction between wildfires and landscape fires. Worsened by extreme weather conditions, wildfires burn with a high intensity that requires extraordinary effort from firefighters. Wildfires can pose significant threats to human communities and to the environment. Landscape fires are much more benign. Often intentionally set, they can benefit ecosystems and promote biodiversity. They burn with low to medium intensity, perhaps with a few periods of higher-intensity flames, and are relatively easy to suppress. Cultural burns and prescribed burns fall into this category. But if such fires spin out of control, they develop into wildfires too.

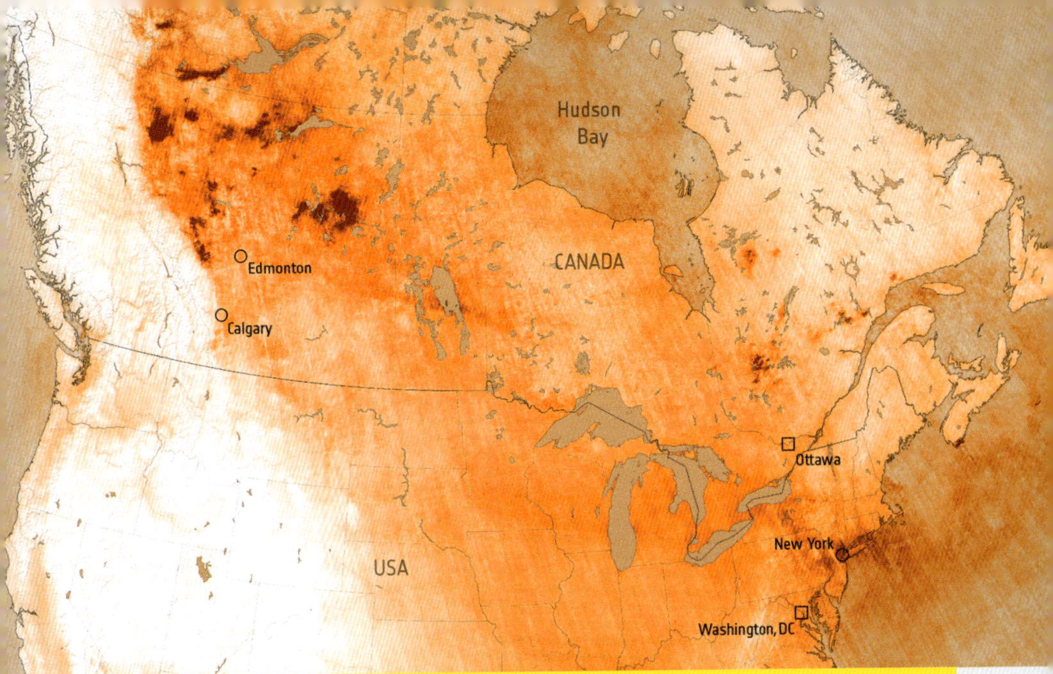

Wildfires can release a lot of harmful particles, causing air pollution. This map shows the concentration of carbon monoxide over Canada and much of the United States between May 1 and June 13, 2023. The darker the color, the higher the concentration. The increase and spread of carbon monoxide during this time was linked to the wildfires in Canada.

When more than five hundred wildfires erupted in Canada between April and June 2023, the international community reacted with deep concern. Although Canada is used to wildfires, it is unusual for fires to burn in both the eastern and western parts of the country at the same time. Because of the tremendous demand on firefighting resources, the government sent military forces to help suppress the flames. Other countries were quick to respond to the Canadian emergency too. Firefighters arrived in Canada from Australia, New Zealand, South Africa, France, Portugal, Spain, and the United States.

By June 8, about 10.6 million acres (4.3 million ha) of land had been scorched. The extent of the burning was about fifteen times greater than the annual average of the previous ten years. Canada's environment and climate minister posted a somber tweet that the fires "remind us that carbon pollution carries a cost on our society, as it accelerates climate change."

The Industrial Revolution and the Greenhouse Effect

Although the speed with which the world is warming and the growing intensity of some fires has surprised many scientists, they have understood the basic mechanics of climate change for many years. Carbon dioxide, a naturally occurring gas in the atmosphere, holds heat. When the sun warms the earth and oceans, some of that energy returns to the atmosphere as heat, or infrared radiation. The gases that make up most of the earth's air, such as oxygen and nitrogen, allow that heat to pass back into space. But CO_2 absorbs the radiation, trapping it in the atmosphere. The higher the concentration of CO_2 in the air, the higher the temperature will rise. Carbon dioxide and other heat-holding gases such as water vapor, methane, nitrous oxide, and ozone intensify heat in the atmosphere just as the glass walls of a greenhouse concentrate heat inside the room. So, those gases are sometimes called greenhouses gases and rising global temperatures, the greenhouse effect.

In recent decades, the amount of CO_2 in the atmosphere has been rising, causing a gradual increase in average global temperatures. This began in the eighteenth century with the Industrial Revolution (1760–1840). Machines replaced many jobs formerly done by human workers. Steam engines powered new machines that turned out products quickly and easily. Within decades, the Industrial Revolution transformed life. But because the steam engines burn fossil fuels such as coal and oil, they emit great amounts of smoke.

The twentieth century saw rapid progress in transportation, manufacturing, and the generation of electricity in power plants. These advances also depended on the burning of fossil fuels, substances that were formed from the remains of prehistoric plants and animals, pressed underground by successive layers of sediment over millions of years. Like all organic matter, fossil fuels contain carbon. When they are burned, their carbon combines with oxygen from the air to form CO_2.

CLIMATE CHANGE PIONEER

A gifted researcher and a vocal advocate for women's rights and suffrage, American scientist Eunice Foote lived in the nineteenth century, a time when women were expected not to pursue scientific interests. But Foote, born July 17, 1819, attended Troy Female Seminary in New York, which encouraged students to attend science classes at a nearby college. After she graduated and married, she followed her natural curiosity by conducting scientific investigations in her home.

In one well-designed experiment, she enclosed a mercury thermometer in each of two glass cylinders. After pumping one cylinder full of air and the other full of CO_2, she placed both in direct sunlight. She found that the container with the CO_2 became much more heated than the other one. When she removed the cylinders from the sunlight, the one with CO_2 took much longer to cool off. Foote understood that her simple experiment had profound implications. In 1856 Foote wrote, "An atmosphere of that gas CO_2 would give to our earth a high temperature."

Foote's work came three years before Irish scientist John Tyndall published his well-known paper on greenhouse gases. As a woman and an amateur scientist, Foote did not receive the recognition she deserved. But in 2011 retired geologist Raymond Sorenson discovered her experiment while rummaging through some old scientific documents and announced her groundbreaking work.

Foote's scientific work was one of the earliest demonstrations of the greenhouse effect.

Tipping Point

As aviation, the automobile industry, and the demand for electrical power grew in the twentieth century, the quantity of CO_2 released into the air skyrocketed. By June 2022, the amount was more than 50 percent greater than in the early 1800s. The heat that excess CO_2 holds is causing the average global temperature to rise more rapidly than many scientists expected. Since the beginning of the Industrial Revolution, temperatures have already risen by 1.8°F (1°C). Experts warn that a tipping point exists where if the earth's average global temperature rises by 3.6°F (2°C), or double what it already has, over preindustrial measurements (or even rises to a lesser degree), it may become impossible to stop climate change. If that happened, events already set in motion such as glaciers and ice sheets melting in the Arctic and Antarctica would spiral out of control with devastating consequences for the entire world.

As the global temperature increases and Arctic sea ice melts, the temperature difference between usually icy polar regions and warmer regions further south shrinks. This destabilizes the polar jet stream and forces the polar vortex, a large area of cold air and low pressure surrounding the North Pole, to expand and move south, bringing severe cold to areas not used to those temperatures. Precipitation that usually falls as rain becomes snow or ice, which people in warmer climates may not be prepared to deal with. Extreme precipitation events such as blizzards can cause power outages, freeze water lines, block roadways, and more, making it difficult for people to stay warm, access supplies, or evacuate if needed. If climate changes worsens, severe cold and winter storms could also become more common.

Continued climate change would increase other types of severe weather too. Since warm air can hold more moisture than colder air, rainfalls would become heavier. Extreme tropical storms and the added sea surge due to higher ocean levels would cause widespread flooding and destruction. Rising sea levels would overwhelm small island

Pratap Nagar village in Bangladesh is one of many places already experiencing severe effects of climate change that may eventually displace many people. Residents face rising water levels and flooding, erosion, and more.

nations and coastal cities. Forced to leave their homes, climate migrants would be severely challenged to find a stable environment in which to live. And this is already happening to many people. Climate and weather risks displaced 30 million people within their own countries in 2020. It is estimated that the number of climate migrants could rise to 1.2 billion by 2050.

Soaring temperatures and droughts, as well as more intense storms, would also cause major crop failures and food shortages. Excessive heat would likely lower the nutritional value of fruits and vegetables. Competition for access to fresh water, arable (suitable) land for farming, and quality grazing ground could ultimately lead to violence and warfare.

How Climate Change Affects Fires

The trend toward a longer fire season and more intense fires is well established. A group of scientists discussed why this is by suggesting a slightly altered fire triangle in 2012. Instead of fuel, heat, and oxygen, they spoke of "resources to burn, atmospheric conditions, and ignitions." Climate change affects all three factors in the following ways:

Resources influence the density and type of vegetation in a specific locale.

Atmospheric conditions consist of daily weather such as temperature, clouds, humidity, and rain. These factors can be influenced by climate change-induced droughts and heat waves.

Ignition is most commonly caused by lightning strikes. According to University of California, Berkeley, professor David Romps's 2014

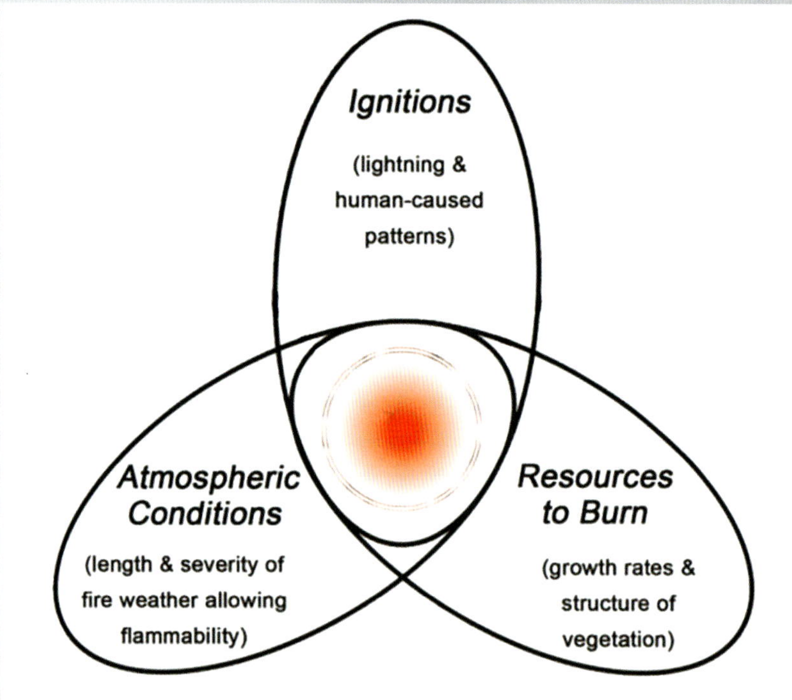

The modified fire triangle helps explain the lengthening fire season and climate change's effect on it.

study, climate change will likely increase the number of lightning strikes. For each degree the global temperature rises, he estimates an almost 7 percent increase in the number of lightning strikes. Other scientists predict that temperatures could rise 7°F (3.9°C) by 2100.

THE FIVE Rs

Every continent except Antarctica is subject to wildfires. According to the United Nations Environment Programme, most regions have a season in which the landscape is especially susceptible to fire. Digital climate change models show that even the Arctic, which experienced little fire in the past, is at risk for future wildfires. Globally, scientists predict an increase in extreme fires of up to 14 percent by 2030, 33 percent by 2050, and 52 percent by 2100. Developing countries, as well as low-income and disadvantaged communities in all countries, may be the most severely impacted because they lack the economic resources to rebuild after an extreme fire.

Acknowledging that advances in firefighting technology are not enough to suppress all dangerous wildfires, the United Nations calls for "integrated wildfire management [as the] key to adapting to current and future changes in global wildfire risk." They sum up this management as the 5Rs: "review and analysis, risk reduction, readiness, response, and recovery."

Communities that take such planning and preventive measures can save more lives and property, execute safe evacuations, designate shelters, and identify places that need to be especially defended such as hospitals or main roads. Although the danger of wildfires cannot be completely eliminated, the impact can be reduced if communities and local governments work together to implement effective precautions.

If this proves true, the twenty-second century could see a 50 percent increase in lightning strikes, leading to many more wildfires.

Because the effects of climate change differ from place to place, some areas may actually experience cooler temperatures and fewer fires than their historical norms. But this too can also be harmful. As atmospheric scientist Katharine Hayhoe explains: "Increases and decreases [in the amount of fire] can both be bad for the natural ecosystem, because wildfire is part of what makes it healthy."

Carbon Emissions from Fire

Environmental changes brought about by climate change, such as droughts, higher temperatures, high winds, lower humidity, and dry lightning affect the length of the fire season and the intensity of flames. In turn, wildfires emit CO_2. Some scientists believe this feedback loop contributes significantly to climate change. Brendan Byrne, a postdoctoral researcher at NASA, as well as other researchers from Australia, New Zealand, and the United States, have used data from satellites that monitor atmospheric levels of CO_2 and other greenhouse gases to estimate how much CO_2 the devastating bushfires that swept across Australia from October 2019 through January 2020 released. According to their calculations, the fires burned more than 65,000 square miles (168,400 sq. km) of land and discharged about 186 million tons (168.7 million t) of carbon into the atmosphere. That is more carbon than Australia's industries release in an entire year of burning fossil fuels.

Under normal conditions, it would take about twenty years for newly sprouting trees and vegetation to absorb all the carbon emitted by these fires. But Byrne wonders about the landscape's ability to

The Australian bushfires swept through huge swaths of vegetation and trees. Some researchers wonder if wildfires of that magnitude make it difficult for the landscape to absorb the carbon emissions they release.

reabsorb vast amounts of carbon. "It's getting warmer and drier, so it can take longer to recover from fires," he said, "plus, you're having more fires. That's a concern that we're causing permanent carbon losses in these [severely burned] areas." With increasingly arid conditions and less vegetation to soak it back in, carbon released by these wildfires may have nowhere to go but into the atmosphere.

Some researchers take a more hopeful view. Ecologist and author Chad Hanson believes the amount of greenhouse gases that the Australian bushfires emitted has been overestimated, an error he thinks has also been made in analyzing fires in Asia, Africa, and North and South America. In his book *Smokescreen*, Hanson discusses field studies

CARBON DIOXIDE REMOVAL TECHNOLOGIES

Carbon dioxide can stay in the atmosphere for hundreds to thousands of years. To avoid the worst effects of climate change, carbon already in the atmosphere will need to be removed. In 2018 the Intergovernmental Panel on Climate Change set forth ways to do this. One natural method is planting more trees.

A variety of technological methods are also being explored. Bioenergy with carbon capture and storage involves burning vegetation in power plants, capturing the CO_2 emitted, and storing it, perhaps by injecting it into the ground. Capturing and storing it prevents the carbon that was previously stored in the vegetation from entering the atmosphere, and burning the vegetation provides carbon neutral energy. In carbon mineralization, scientists utilize a natural process by combining reactive substances such as peridotite or basaltic lava with CO_2-bearing fluid. The substances bond with the carbon to form carbonate minerals such as limestone, which can hold carbon for millions of years. The fluid containing CO_2 can be combined with the reactive materials at carbon capture stations or pumped into naturally occurring rock formations. Another technology, direct air capture, uses fans to blow air across substances that will chemically bind with the CO_2 in the air, preventing the CO_2 from reentering the atmosphere. In enhanced weathering, scientists accelerate a natural process by which rocks and soil react with atmospheric CO_2 to form bicarbonate. This is done by spreading crushed rock on the land or sea. The bicarbonate is carried to the ocean, where it remains.

Kate Gordon, a fellow at the Columbia Center on Global Energy Policy, cautions that no one approach will solve the climate crisis. "We need to reduce emissions dramatically," she said, "we need to come up with more renewable energy options to replace fossil fuels, we need to electrify a lot of things that are currently run on petroleum and then we need to do an enormous amount of carbon removal."

showing that substantially fewer numbers of trees burned in Australia than had been assumed by many researchers. He is also optimistic about the ability of forests to reabsorb carbon quickly. "Forests," he writes, "respond within days or weeks after a fire passes, absorbing an accelerating amount of carbon from the atmosphere and storing it in the new, rapidly growing postfire shrubs and trees. This process is aided by the nutrient-rich bed of mineral ash."

Together with ecologists Mark Harmon and Dominick DellaSala, Hanson investigated areas in the western United States that had experienced recent fires. In a four-year field study sponsored by Oregon State University, they analyzed the rates at which different parts of the forest burned, including branches, individual trees, stands that included different types and sizes of trees and, finally, the landscape as a whole. The researchers found that small branches and fragments of large trees as well as 57 percent of small trees burned completely, but this was not the full story. Looking at stands of trees, the researchers found that only 0.1 to 3.2 percent of those trees had been destroyed. Going beyond individual groups of trees to look at the entire area burned by the fires, the numbers were even lower, between 0.6 to 1.8 percent. If the researchers' numbers are correct, much less carbon enters the atmosphere from forest fires than people previously believed. And many more trees survive wildfires.

More detailed studies are required to determine the extent to which wildfires contribute to climate change, a finding that may impact forest management. But the burning of fossil fuels—the industrial fire of power plants, factories, and the transportation industry—is the chief driver of climate change. Many people argue that we should transition to green sources of energy, such as solar panels and wind farms. By lessening the amount of carbon in the atmosphere and helping to control climate change, green energy also makes the hot, dry conditions that foster severe wildfires less likely. Transitioning to green sources of energy not only benefits the climate, but it also reduces the risk of uncontrollable wildfires.

IF ADAPTATION IS TO BE OUR FUTURE

Gustavo Petro, president of Colombia, never forgot the wisdom an Indigenous leader shared with him. "Oil is the blood of Mother Earth," Roberto Cobaría (originally named Berito Kuwaru'wa), leader of the U'wa, told Petro. Then Cobaría issued a chilling warning: extracting oil from the ground would ultimately destroy life. About forty years later, in May 2023, Petro stood before the United Nations Permanent Forum on Indigenous Issues and shared these profound words. Cobaría had been proved correct. Burning oil and other fossil fuels had led to increased temperatures and climate change, an existential threat to the whole world.

Managing about 80 percent of the world's biodiversity, Indigenous peoples are especially vulnerable to ecological changes. According to Meade Krosby, a conservation biologist at the University of Washington, they "have unique connections to the land and are feeling the impacts the earliest and most severely."

But although they are the hardest hit, Indigenous peoples have a

Roberto Cobaría at a protest against oil drilling in 1997. Much of his work focused on stopping oil drilling, especially on the traditional homelands of the U'wa people.

Ferin Davis Anderson uses controlled burning during the Puzzle Fire on Rosebud reservation in 2020. Burning low vegetation creates a buffer that helps prevent the spread of wildfire.

deeply ingrained resourcefulness and centuries of knowledge to help them adapt to the changing environment and fight climate change. For example, the Karuk in Northern California call for prescribed burns to lessen the chances of a fire spinning out of control. The Confederated Salish and Kootenai Tribes in Montana also advocate for prescribed burns and fostering the comeback of whitebark pine trees.

The Swinomish of the North American West Coast was the very first Indigenous tribe to issue a climate policy. They have returned to ancient practices to increase the numbers of shellfish in coastal waters, boosting an important food supply. In 2007 the Swinomish announced that they would study the impacts of climate change, and a climate action plan followed in 2010. M. Brian Cladoosby, chair of the Swinomish Indian Senate, rallied his community in the written forward to the plan. "What we have achieved is only the first step in what we expect to be a long and demanding journey into an uncertain future, a future that all signs indicate may be much different from what we know today. . . . If adaptation is to be our future, we at Swinomish have already proved ourselves equal to the challenge." Since the publication of the Swinomish climate plan, fifty Native American tribes have followed suit by developing strategies to safeguard their environments and cultures.

CHAPTER SIX

Fire Creating Its Own Weather

THE INCREASE OF HIGH-INTENSITY FIRES, WHICH SEND PLUMES of smoke high into the atmosphere, has ushered in a new age of what is sometimes called megafires. Defined by their size and impact, megafires may blaze through a million or more acres. Sparks exploding from the forest canopy may soar to heights two-and-one-half times higher than the tree itself. Propelled by high winds, these sparks can land miles away, igniting new fires.

Pyrocumulonimbus clouds can form over heat sources such as fires. They are recognizable by their distinct shape and often-towering height.

The Dixie Fire: Anatomy of a Firestorm

Weather, specifically heat waves and droughts, can increase the likelihood that a fire will spin out of control. In turn, megafires change atmospheric conditions, creating their own extreme weather. This happened with the Dixie Fire, which ignited in Northern California in mid-July 2021. In less than a week, the flames consumed over 30,000 acres (12,150 ha) of forest lands. Plentiful layers of dry vegetation fed the conflagration, accelerating its momentum. On July 19, towering columns of smoke rose into the air—a firestorm was in the making. As the air grew hotter, it began to expand upward in strong gusts of wind. Water vapor condensed on particles of ash from the smoke, forming bulky pyrocumulus (from the Greek *pyro* for fire and Latin *cumulus* for heap) clouds. Rapidly, the clouds intensified into pyrocumulonimbus (from the Latin *nimbus* for rain cloud) clouds, generally shortened to pyroCb. NASA calls pyroCbs the "fire-breathing dragon of clouds."

The distinctively anvil-shaped clouds can soar more than 40,000 feet (12,200 m), spawning lightning and high winds.

Rain plunged down from the pyroCb, but much of it was absorbed into the atmosphere before it hit the ground. Hot winds propelled the flames forward, which may have generated another pyroCb cloud. Eventually, the clouds finally began to dispel, but the Dixie Fire blazed on until October and continued to provoke more storms.

When the fire was almost contained, the *New York Times* published a 3D-augmented reality experience that allowed people to visualize the magnitude of the disaster. The 3D map let viewers follow the fire's first thunderclouds and offered additional information about when, where, and how they formed. The powerful imagery helped viewers understand how the Dixie Fire burned almost 1 million acres (404,680 ha) and destroyed several communities. Smoke drifted as far away as Utah and Colorado, prompting air-quality alerts. More than $637 million was spent to counter the blaze over the four months that it burned. It was the most expensive fire ever fought in the United States, as well as the largest fire in the history of California.

Tornadoes Made of Fire

Standing on his back deck in Wanniassa, Australia, in January 2003, Jim Venn took an amazing (and terrifying) photo. A ferocious wildfire burned in the distance, but the tall, rapidly twisting cone Venn observed was different from the rest of the blaze. It looked like an enormous funnel, but it was made of smoke and fire. Venn had never seen anything like it. Later, scientists would mathematically analyze the photo, which turned out to be the world's first recorded fire tornado. Its updraft speed (the speed at which it could lift things up) was determined to be between 124 and 155 miles (200 to 250 km) per hour. The fire tornado (also recorded on video) touched down six times and lifted a 15,000-pound (6,800 kg) roof from a water tower and deposited it 0.5 miles (0.8 km) away.

LIGHTNING FACTS

Lightning can travel from one cloud to another or from a cloud to the earth.

Lightning piercing the sky during a thunderstorm is a dazzling sight. It begins high in the atmosphere when cold temperatures freeze droplets of moisture in the clouds. As the small specks of ice collide with one another in the turbulent air, electrons are knocked off some particles and added to others. Those that gain extra electrons become negatively charged while those that lose electrons become positively charged. Over time, the positively charged particles accumulate at the top of the cloud. Negative charges collect at the bottom of the cloud. This creates an imbalance between the clouds and the surface of the earth, which carries a positive charge. As more and more negative electrons amass, the attraction between them and the positive ground reaches the breaking point. A current of electricity passes from the cloud to the earth, a phenomenon we observe as a flash of lightning.

A burst of lightning can heat the air to around 90,000°F (50,000°C), five times as hot as the surface of the sun. The intense heat makes the air unstable, causing the air to vibrate and expand rapidly into a roaring sound wave, or boom of thunder.

Here are a few more interesting facts about lightning:

- A flash of lightning is only about 1 inch (2.5 cm) wide.
- Lightning travels at about 62,000 miles (99,780 km) per second.
- Satellite data reveals that lightning flashes in the atmosphere more than 4.3 million times every day. That means it flashes about 50 times every second.
- The safest place to be when lightning flashes is indoors. If you are outdoors, avoid tall trees, poles, water, and anything metal such as a bicycle. Try to keep away from open areas.

Extremely rare, fire tornadoes (sometimes called firenadoes) can occur when the intense heat of a fire causes air to rise into the atmosphere. As the air accelerates upward from the blaze, it leaves an

THE WORDS WE USE

No one denies that an uncontained fire can cause catastrophe. The loss of human life and property, as well as endangering wildlife species, are absolute disasters. It has also been well established that climate change is lengthening the fire season and increasing the intensity of certain fires. But some ecologists feel the term *catastrophic wildfire* has been overused and promotes fear and misunderstanding. They believe that some people use the term in a politically motivated way and that it misrepresents the science of fire. Accustomed to hearing fire described solely in terms of devastation, many people don't realize the importance of fire in maintaining a healthy ecology.

Rhetoric in the media also seems to suggest that fire is more prevalent in the United States now than in the past. But ecologist Hanson believes there were more fires in North America before colonists arrived than there are today. According to estimates, 20 to 30 million acres (8.1 million to 12.1 million ha) burned annually before Europeans began settling in the West. In the twenty-first century, only 4 to 5 million acres (1.6 million to 2 million ha) burn each year.

"The term catastrophic wildfire is scientifically bankrupt," Hanson said, "there is no question about it. It has no scientific credibility." He also asserts that words such as *megafire* and *uncharacteristic wildfire* also carry negative connotations that can prejudice people against the need for fire.

A fire whirl rises from the Pine Gulch Fire in Colorado in 2020.

area of low pressure behind. More air rushes in from all directions to restore the pressure. While this new air is also rising, shear winds (winds that travel in different directions) moving across the landscape can cause the air, smoke, and fire to spin rapidly in a vortex.

More common than fire tornadoes, smaller fire whirls are often spotted in wildfires, sometimes a dozen or more. These swirling funnels of fire generally measure anywhere from a few feet (about 1 m) to 1,500 feet (457 m) in diameter. The larger ones are as strong as a small tornado. Fire tornadoes can vary in intensity from slight to powerful enough to tear 16-inch (41 cm) branches from oak trees.

According to Jason Forthofer, a firefighter and mechanical engineer with the Forest Service, the difference between fire tornadoes and fire whirls is one of degree. "Fire tornadoes are . . . the larger version of a fire whirl," he explained, "and they are . . . really the size and scale of a regular tornado." In his research at the Missoula Fire Sciences Lab in Montana, the largest such facility in the world, Forthofer has simulated fire whirls in 12-foot-tall (3.7 m) tubes. After pouring alcohol into the bottom of the tube, he lights a flame. As the fire heats the air, it rises, spilling out over the top of the tube. Cooler air rushes downward to equalize the pressure at the bottom. The continuous stream of moving air in opposite directions sets the fire spinning—which mimics what happens in nature.

ZOMBIE FIRES

Sander Veraverbeke, an earth scientist at Vrije Universiteit of Amsterdam in the Netherlands, was puzzled as he compared images from two fire seasons in Alaska and Canada. One year after some fires had been extinguished, new fires had erupted in almost the same locations as the earlier blazes. Veraverbeke knew it couldn't be a coincidence, and he was determined to find out what was happening. One possibility especially intrigued him. Contacting fire managers in the areas where they had observed the flames, he asked if it is possible for fires to smolder underground for the winter and emerge again in the spring. The answer was yes! Such fires are popularly called zombie fires because they seem to rise from the dead like their science fiction counterparts, but many experts call them overwintering or holdover fires.

Relatively rare occurring zombie fires are generally responsible for less than 1 percent of the burned area in the boreal forest of the Far North. But the amount can vary considerably from year to year. For example, in 2008 one zombie fire burned about 53 square miles (137 sq. km) in Alaska and comprised over one-third of the total area burned that year in the state. But climate change may be causing an increase in this phenomenon. Warming more quickly than the rest

Studying small fire whirls helps Forthofer understand how full-blown fire tornadoes develop in the wild and may provide information that saves lives. "Hopefully we can provide firefighters with enough training to—as soon as [fire tornadoes are] forming—get out of the way."

of the world, the Arctic is experiencing melting glaciers, diminished snow, hotter summers, and a longer fire season. The number of Arctic wildfires, caused by lightning or human accident, has risen steadily for over twenty years. Scientists say that fires are more frequent in the twenty-first century than any time since boreal forests reached their modern state around three thousand years ago and may even be more frequent in that region than any time in the last ten thousand years. A larger number of these apparently extinguished fires may also be reappearing as zombie with the return of warmer weather.

Locked in a feedback loop, climate change is indirectly linked to the number of zombie fires, but these fires also contribute to climate change by emitting CO_2. Because the soils in which they smolder are often composed of peat—which contains a massive amount of carbon—zombie fires emit more CO_2 than most other wildfires. Almost 4 million acres (1.6 million ha) of Arctic lands are covered by peatlands that store about 415 gigatons (415 billion t) of carbon, the same amount that all the trees in the world can store. Zombie fires thaw layers of permafrost. Even after a fire is extinguished, decaying organic matter in the permafrost can continue to release greenhouse gases for decades.

CHAPTER SEVEN

Fire Heroes: Confronting the Blaze

ISOLATED ON A RISE OF LAND, BRENDAN MCDONOUGH SERVED AS the lookout while his fellow firefighters dug a ditch to contain the swiftly approaching flames. The town of Yarnell, Arizona, population about 650, lay directly in the path of the fire. Ignited by lightning on June 28, 2013, and fueled by dense, dry vegetation that had not burned in forty-five years, the fire grew rapidly. On June 30,

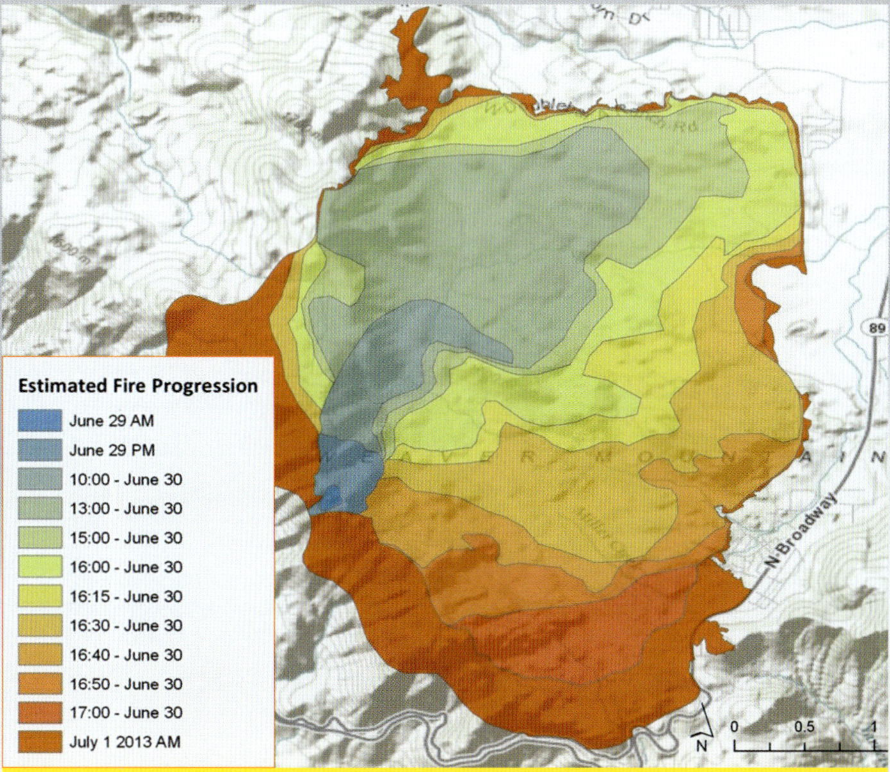

The Yarnell Hill Fire spread quickly. This map estimates how the fire progressed between the mornings of June 29 and July 1.

the town's residents were told to evacuate within three hours, but a sudden shift in the winds intensified the emergency. They had to gather their things and leave within half an hour.

The Granite Mountain Hotshots, an elite and dedicated team of wilderness firefighters, headed into the mountains that morning. The wind and steep terrain put the hotshots in an extremely dangerous situation. A National Weather Service employee warned that the area's rocky, rough landscape would have a major impact on the fire's trajectory.

From his vantage point, McDonough radioed his crew that his position had become too dangerous. Only one option was left to

A memorial to the Granite Mountain Hotshots stands in Arizona. The Yarnell Hill Fire and the death of the hotshots demonstrated the risks wildfires can pose.

him—a ditch that had been dug to serve as an escape route. Making his way through the trench as quickly as he could, he glanced back and discovered that his previous location was already on fire.

McDonough never saw his nineteen crewmates again. Later that day, their bodies were discovered in a steep basin. Some of them were within the emergency shelters they had deployed to protect themselves from the smoke and soaring heat of the fire. But temperatures exceeding 2,000°F (1,093°C) had rendered the shelters useless. It was the single largest loss of firefighters since the terrorist attacks of September 11, 2001.

Thousands of people attended their memorial service on July 9, 2013, including representatives from more than a hundred hotshot teams and then vice president Joe Biden. "Firefighting is not what they did," Biden said, struggling to keep his voice steady. "It was who they were."

A smoke jumper parachutes down over Missoula, Montana.

Hotshots, Smoke Jumpers, and Helitack Crews

The Yarnell Hill Fire demonstrated the deep risks wildfires pose to the environment, human communities, and firefighters alike. In confronting out-of-control blazes, firefighters have a variety of roles to play. Twenty-person hotshot crews, rigorously trained to suppress flames in some of the harshest conditions imaginable, remain on call, day and night, throughout the wildfire season. Hotshots set up camps in safe locations, dig fire lines to contain the flames, and clear away tangled vegetation that could feed the approaching fire. Hotshots have been known to call their work "the best and worst job I've ever had."

Like hotshots, smoke jumper candidates must undergo long, difficult training. Parachuting from planes about 3,000 feet (914 m) high into remote areas, they carry about 85 pounds (39 kg) of gear, including some firefighting tools. After they land, more equipment such as sleeping bags, chain saws, and water is parachuted to them. They are often able to reach a fire while it's still relatively small and easier to contain. Their tasks include chopping trees, digging ditches, and clearing vegetation to create firebreaks. There are about 450 smoke jumpers in the United States located across nine bases.

Hotshots have been known to call their work "the best and worst job I've ever had."

Helitack teams arrive via helicopter. They may land near the wildfire or, if properly equipped and experienced, they may rappel from the helicopter as it hovers overhead. Using chain saws and other firefighting tools, they build fire lines to stop the flames. Helitack crews also deliver equipment and people where they are needed and may create helispots (helicopter landing spots) with easier access to the fire for other incoming crew members.

Although hotshots, smoke jumpers, and helitack crews are especially well known, other types of fire crews also contribute to the successful suppression of wildfires and the careful monitoring of prescribed burns. Many different skills come together to protect the country's wildlands.

I Wanted to Change Things

Often working twelve hours a day or longer, wildland firefighters confront fires as closely as they safely can, manage controlled burns meant to create firebreaks, and follow in the fire's wake to extinguish spots continuing to smolder. Stationed at base camps for weeks at a time, they inhale heavily contaminated air. Despite exhaustion, heat, and unavoidable danger, they push themselves to contain the blaze.

McDonough, the only survivor of the Granite Mountain Hotshots, has thought a lot about these conditions. "I wanted to change things," he wrote in his book, *My Lost Brothers: The Untold Story of Yarnell Hill Fire's Lone Survivor*. "How can we make it safer out there?"

McDonough answers his question by calling for improved communication between hotshots and supervisors. In extreme circumstances, a GPS and radio contact may not be enough. He explained that no one thinks about radioing their position in the field when confronting a violent megafire. Firefighters are concerned instead about "living for the next 120 seconds." McDonough thinks all hotshots should have a Satellite Emergency Notification Device (SEND). The small device would continuously transmit a hotshot's location to a supervisor who also has access to data about the fire's trajectory. The supervisor could alert firefighters of changes in the fire's direction, giving them a chance to get away before the flames overtake them. Although the Forest Service purchased thousands of SENDs in 2012, the Granite Mountain Hotshots didn't have any when they battled the blaze at Yarnell Hill. McDonough would also like to see more tanker planes, helicopters, and firefighters put into service. "The more resources you put into a wildfire, the safer it is for everyone."

SMART FIREFIGHTING: ROBOTS, DRONES, AND ARTIFICIAL INTELLIGENCE

The first robotic firefighting vehicle in the United States, the Thermite RS3, was late to its public unveiling in 2020. While en route to the press conference where it was to be displayed for the first time, it was rerouted to a structure fire that broke out in downtown Los Angeles. The large building contained heaps of fabric. Pushing through mounds of burning cloth, the 3,500-pound (1,588 kg) Thermite RS3 made a pathway for firefighters to safely enter the building.

Although robots will not replace human firefighters, they can endure high temperatures and dense smoke that could be fatal to humans. They can vary from the size of a child's wagon to a military tank. In a single minute, larger robots can release 2,500 gallons (9,460 L) of water. Researchers are working on robots that can even act on their own instead of being remote-controlled.

Many other technologies are being developed to help and protect firefighters. Thermal imaging cameras allow firefighters to see objects in dense smoke. When equipped with a camera, drones, which firefighters often called unmanned aerial systems, can provide important photos of the scene that fire chiefs use when allocating resources. At night they can focus floodlights on the ground to increase visibility for firefighters. They can even deliver needed supplies such as parachutes, blankets, radio devices, or life preservers. The Forest Service employs special drones that can stay in the air for a month and report signs or evidence of wildfire. Drones can also be equipped with dragon eggs—small spheres filled with chemicals that are dropped to the ground to ignite small fires that burn potential fuel. During the Dixie Fire in 2021, the Forest Service used drones to slowly drop these spheres down a steep terrain to burn debris that would otherwise further feed the fire.

The Thermite RS3 sprays water during a demonstration. This and other robots can help firefighters do their job and keep them safer from fire conditions.

Space-age technology is also important. Satellites from the National Oceanic and Atmospheric Administration can detect wildfires in remote locations before anyone on the ground discovers them. They provide real-time data about the fire's size and temperature. This information is vital to firefighters and first responders. Satellites also enable scientists to follow the trajectory of the smoke more accurately.

Artificial intelligence has made some promising developments in helping suppress wildfires too. Smart technologies that analyze the landscape, weather, and other factors from past fires can help firefighters make the safest decisions and establish evacuation plans.

Smaller firefighting helicopters can carry 100 to 400 gallons (378.5 to 1,514 L) of water or retardant in buckets beneath the aircraft.

Aerial Fire Suppression

An air tanker dropping a load of red fire retardant to contain a blaze is an impressive sight. Airplanes and helicopters can fly over rocky steep terrains, difficult for ground crews to navigate, and they serve a variety of purposes. For example, aerial cranes, helicopters fitted with enormous vats, are equipped with a long suction hose, or snorkel, that hangs from the water supply. The snorkel allows the vat to be refilled from a lake or other body of water without the helicopter having to land. Other types of helicopters, sometimes called helibuckets or helitorches, have a hanging basket, which the pilot operates to drop water or fire retardant. And some helicopters have flamethrowers that dangle about 25 feet (7.6 m) below the aircraft. The pilot can use the flamethrower to start fuel moving through a nozzle. A special device ignites the fuel, which falls to the earth as strings of fire. In this way, firefighters backburn land (create firebreaks) to deprive a wildfire of fuel when it reaches the newly burned area.

Many types of fixed-wing aircraft, from large, military-style planes to smaller, commercial aircraft, are also used to suppress fire. The DC-10 tanker, one of the largest aircraft firefighters use, can hold up to 12,000 gallons (45,425 L) of retardant or water. Sometimes spotter planes circle the area and radio to the tankers the best places to drop retardant or water. Pilots also keep in close contact with the crew on the ground.

The aim of aerial firefighting is not to extinguish the blaze but to assist the ground crew. "It is the men and women with boots on the ground (with cooperation from nature) that put fires out; we only operate in support of the ground crews. We act to slow or hold fires so that the ground crews can get them under control," Canadian firefighting pilot Dennis Chrystian said.

In the air, as on the ground, firefighters face great danger. Aircraft must fly low to reach their targets, but smoke and high winds, often from the fire itself, make it hazardous to fly close to a wildfire. Between

Aerial fire retardants are usually colored red or orange to help firefighters see where they've been dropped on a landscape.

2005 and 2015, thirty-seven aerial firefighters died in accidents. The Forest Service determined that if firefighters on the ground had about the same casualty rate, over two hundred would die each year.

Debate over Fire Retardant

Since the late 1950s, aircraft have been dumping retardant around blazes in the United States to stop fires. Phos-Chek, one of the most widely used retardants in the US, consists of 80 percent water, 10 percent of the fertilizer solution ammonium phosphate, and 10 percent of various ingredients to color and thicken the retardant and prevent corrosion. When fire draws near a line of Phos-Chek, the heat triggers a release of water vapor from the retardant. The water vapor slows the fire's advance and lowers the ground temperature. This permits firefighters to approach and attack the flames more effectively.

For many years, no concrete data existed on the effectiveness of retardants in aerial firefighting. According to experiments conducted by the Forest Service into the early 2000s, retardants lessen fire intensity and slow its progress twice as efficiently as water does. Cecilia

Johnson, a specialist with Wildland Fire Chemical Systems at the Forest Service, also believes that retardant can have a significant impact on wildfire management. "Actual firefighters . . . said that [retardant is] what held this line," she explained. "That's what allowed them to get

A PROFITABLE VENTURE

Between 2012 and 2019, the Forest Service dropped more than 102 million gallons (386 million L) of fire retardant at about two dollars per 1 gallon (3.8 L). Aircraft are expensive too. As of 2023, it cost thousands of dollars per hour to keep an air tanker or helicopter in the sky, not covering the high cost of keeping these aircraft on standby.

Although firefighting is expensive for organizations such as the Forest Service, many make money off it too. In the past, firefighting was primarily a federal job. But now when a wildfire erupts, many private companies provide firefighters as well as equipment and supplies to set up base camps too. Unless they're suppressing a fire, these companies do not make money. Privatizing firefighting gives businesses a reason to lobby for suppressing all fires, even those that ignite in distant wildernesses. Developers who build homes in fire-prone areas also have a financial stake in seeing all blazes suppressed. Despite the increased likelihood of fire, they claim that their subdivisions are safe because firefighters will protect them. The financial interests of private companies that make money from fire suppression places them at odds with fire ecologists who understand that fire is a natural and necessary process with beneficial ecological results.

the crews in in time. It's making our life a lot easier." But more recent reports disagree. A 2011 study from the Forest Service Employees for Environmental Ethics group could not verify the Forest Service's results using the same data. Then a study published in the *International Journal of Wildland Fire* provided even clearer statistics for 2010 and 2011. Fire retardant failed to contain almost 75 percent of the fires on which it was dumped during that time.

One reason might be that fierce gales that drive the retardant away before it can reach its intended destination may lessen its effectiveness. When winds are less severe, retardants may be more successful. But some people, such as Andy Stahl, executive director of Forest Service Employees for Environmental Ethics, argue against using retardant at all. "There's no scientific evidence that it makes any difference in wildfire outcomes," he said. "[Using retardant] is like dumping cash out of airplanes, except that it's toxic and you can't buy anything with it because it doesn't work."

MONTANA LAWSUIT

A 2023 federal lawsuit in Montana tried to stop the Forest Service from dropping retardant over waterways. The Forest Service claimed that that would prevent them from using any retardant at all and that retardant is essential in suppressing fire. But the people filing the lawsuit pointed out that the Forest Service could widen no-retardant buffer zones along streams, rivers, and other bodies of water instead. In May a judge ruled that firefighters could continue to use retardant despite the pollution it introduces to bodies of water. The lawsuit was just the latest in an ongoing series of legal battles.

When retardant misses its target, the results can also be ecologically damaging. As of 2023, air tankers had dumped more than 760,000 gallons (2,876,900 L) of fire retardant into water. Some of the drops were accidental. Others were intentional because the Forest Service determined they would lessen the danger to humans. Concentrated levels of retardant in ponds, streams, and other bodies of water promote the growth of algae blossoms that can harm or even kill amphibians, fish, and other aquatic plants and animals. For example, the use of retardant to suppress a California fire in 2009 resulted in the deaths of dozens of steelhead trout, an endangered species.

Human health is also a consideration in the debate over fire retardant. As more fires come close to human settlements, more communities encounter fire retardant. Though not considered a serious health risk for humans, it can cause breathing problems and irritate eyes and skin.

Many questions remain about whether retardant is effective and should be used. Some scientists wonder whether retardant might cause other long-term effects on people, if it affects the crops people and animals later eat, and even whether it may fertilize invasive plants and lead to more fuel for future fires.

Smoke Hazards

When the Canada wildfires began in 2023, the smoke spread so far that US communities stretching from Vermont south to South Carolina and west to Ohio and Kansas felt the effects. Visibility was so poor in New York in early June that La Guardia Airport canceled flights. The city's schools canceled classes. Health officials strongly recommended limiting outdoor activities, especially cautioning that children, older adults, and those with breathing or heart issues were particularly at risk. They recommended wearing masks to those who had to be outdoors.

The health risk from wildfire air pollution has grown steadily worse over the past decade. Between 2016 and 2020, the number of days California experienced severe wildfires more than doubled, exposing its residents to increased air pollution. Most of the danger from wildfire comes from the microscopic particles suspended in the smoke and haze. Particles 2.5 micrometers in diameter or smaller (known as PM2.5) are especially dangerous. By comparison, an average human hair is 50 to 70 micrometers wide. PM2.5 particles are tiny enough to settle deep in the lungs and even enter the bloodstream. Their presence increases the risk of lung cancer or heart disease. Wildfires and combustion-related events are not the only cause of particle pollution and the PM2.5 it contains but, according to the Environmental Protection Agency, they are the most common.

Firefighters must wear heavy protective equipment to stay safe from fire and smoke.

Exposed to smoke on a regular basis, firefighters face a difficult dilemma. They need protection from the pollution, such as masks, but their job requires energy and alertness. "[Firefighters'] respiratory demands are similar to those people engaging in athletic events," according to Mike DeGrosky, chief of the Fire Protection Bureau with the Montana Department of Natural Resources and Conservation. "You put any kind of restrictive thing over your nose and mouth and you're decreasing your oxygen update, which decreases your muscle abilities [and] your cognitive abilities." Hotshots, smoke jumpers, and ground crews work to the point of exhaustion.

Sometimes, Those Risks All Add Up

It's hard to know what changes can realistically be implemented to mitigate firefighters' health and safety risks. About a year after the tragedy at Yarnell Hill, a reporter asked Bill Morse, a fire captain in Flagstaff, Arizona, a difficult question. The reporter wanted to know if the outcome at Yarnell Hill had affected the more aggressive tactics employed on a recent fire. Morse took his time answering. "Firefighter and public safety have always been our No. 1 concern," he assured everyone. Decisions could be difficult, and risks were inevitable. "Sometimes, those risks all add up," Morse continued. "Sometimes, all of those factors come together at once, and that's what happened at Yarnell. We didn't really learn anything new. We knew all the basics. But maybe our attitude as firefighters is going to be safer." The legacy of Yarnell Hill may simply be to increase the caution with which hotshots and other firefighters confront a blaze.

CHAPTER EIGHT

Learning to Use and to Live with Fire

THE HELICOPTER HOVERED OVER A SCENE OF DESOLATION. LOOKING down on the 6 square miles (15.5 sq. km) blackened by fire, then Colorado governor John Hickenlooper felt the pain of those whose lives the fire had impacted. "Flying over that and seeing firsthand the level of loss," the governor reflected afterward, "I mean there's nothing left. Just foundations [of houses] in many cases."

Smoke from the Lower North Fork Fire traveled high into the air.

The fire was the Lower North Fork Fire that began in the mountains southwest of Denver on March 26, 2012. Nine hundred homes had to be evacuated, and twenty-three were destroyed. Three people were trapped by the blaze and died.

After his aerial view of the damage, Hickenlooper met with some of the evacuees at a Red Cross shelter. Many of them demanded to know what had happened. Why had the fire grown so large and threatened their community?

Their anger was understandable, and the governor had no easy answers. The Lower North Fork Fire had begun as a state-prescribed burn on March 22 to reduce dried and dead vegetation in an area dense with pine trees. For several days after extinguishing the fire, management crews carefully watched the area. But a remaining stray ember blew beyond the fire's border and kindled a patch of grass. High winds whipped the flames into a fierce blaze, a situation that firefighters call a slop-over—a controlled fire that gains the momentum to go wild.

Although Hickenlooper took the evacuees' concerns and frustrations seriously and had temporarily suspended prescribed burnings the previous day, he also understood the burns' importance in reducing dead vegetation and thinning dense undergrowth. "If we made mistakes, let's figure out what the mistakes were and correct them, have the process better," he said. "If we did everything right, then we have to look at it again and say do we want to change any of those?"

Planning a Prescribed Burn

People must take a variety of factors into consideration before undertaking a prescribed burn. These factors include the speed and direction of the wind, relative humidity (the amount of water vapor in the air), temperature, topography, recent rainfalls, and moisture in the soil. The dampness of the soil is crucial in keeping the roots of grasses and trees from being destroyed. The time of day also influences the fire's behavior. For example, after sunset, air tends to become colder and more humid, making it harder to control the smoke.

Fire managers must also choose to establish firebreaks to keep a fire in check before a burn can begin. These are the four main types of firebreaks: *Natural firebreaks* are topographical features such as streams, lakes, or roads. *Constructed firebreaks* may be areas devoid of vegetation, areas that have been doused with water or fire retardant, or areas that have been mowed frequently to keep dry fuel from building up. *Green-crop firebreaks* use plants with low flammability such as barley, clovers, or winter wheat to keep a fire within bounds. *Black lines* burned into the ground to create an empty area that deprives the fire of fuel.

Despite the strictest precautions, burn crews can't anticipate every possibility. The burn crew must have an emergency plan in case the fire takes an unexpected turn. Then the crew must alert the local fire department and nearby residents, and the crew must be aware of safety zones and escape routes.

Vital Work

Prescribed burns that cross over firebreaks and escape are rare. Randy Moore, chief of the Forest Service, explained the statistics in a public statement in 2022: "We conduct an average of 4,500 prescribed fire projects annually: 99.84 percent go according to plan. That equals slightly more than one escape per every 1,000 prescribed fires, or about six escapes per year. But we can always improve." The few escapes generally do little damage, but in rare instances they have resulted in disaster.

A prescribed burn that the US Forest Service conducted on April 6, 2022, broke through firebreaks as high winds scattered sparks and ignited new blazes. Another prescribed burn nearby had also

Burn crews take many precautions to make prescribed burns safe. New technology such as the BurnBot RX1 is also being developed to help create firebreaks in difficult terrain and conduct prescribed burns.

escaped after smoldering for several months. When the two merged, the Calf Canyon/Hermits Peak Fire grew into the largest wildfire in New Mexico's history. Flames devoured more than nine hundred buildings and blackened about 534 square miles (1,383 sq. km). Tens of thousands of people had to evacuate their homes. The Forest Service later found that the prescribed fire encountered significantly drier conditions than the crew had anticipated.

To prevent future calamities and to deal with growing public anger, Moore called a ninety-day halt to prescribed burning beginning

COMPUTER MODELS FOR PRESCRIBED BURNS

Conditions have to be perfect for a safe, successful prescribed burn. If the wind shifts suddenly or an area of vegetation is drier than expected, a crew may lose control, resulting in tragedy. Or smoke may drift to nearby neighborhoods, polluting the air and potentially harming people and animals. Computer models that simulate a proposed burn can help fire managers determine when and where ignitions should take place and how many may be required for the safest, most beneficial outcome. FIRETEC, a tool developed at Los Alamos National Laboratory in New Mexico, uses the principles of physics and research about how substances move to estimate how a fire may behave and react to factors such as the terrain, fuel load, weather, and more. Atmospheric scientist Rodman Linn and fire scientist J. Kevin Hiers called the system "the equivalent of a flight simulator," which is used to train airline pilots for real-life flights.

in May 2022. But while ordering a thorough review of fire practices and protocols, he stressed the need for continued prescribed burns "to improve the health and resilience of our forests and grasslands. That work is vital to reducing the potential for catastrophic wildfires."

In September 2022 the Forest Service resumed its prescribed burning program with additional regulations in place. Many advocates of carefully controlled burning, including some Indigenous leaders, worried that the new, more stringent rules would weaken the vital program. "It's pretty much going to shut burning down at any level significant to what needs to take place, at least in the Forest Service jurisdictions," Bill Tripp of the Karuk Tribe Department of Natural Resources in Northern California explained.

Speaking for the Forest Service, Assistant Director for Media Relations Shayne Martin explained that climate change is causing both prescribed burns and wildfires to act in unexpected ways. "We need prescribed fire to make these communities safe in the long-term," he said, "but it can't come at the expense of safety in the short run."

Just Postponing It

According to the National Interagency Fire Center, 66,255 wildfires ignited in 2022, burning more than 7.5 million acres (3 million ha). The most common natural source for these fires was lightning strikes, but human causes, both deliberate and accidental, accounted for 85 to 90 percent. Arson, carelessly tended campfires, irresponsibly discarded cigarettes, careless burning of trash or leaves, and poorly maintained vehicles or equipment account for most of the blazes.

No one can say how many wildfires burn less intensely because the areas in which they ignite have been purged by controlled burning. But firefighting agencies must decide what to do about these unplanned blazes. If a fire does not threaten any human communities, should they allow it to burn out naturally, or should they suppress it? The call can be a tough one. The Forest Service no longer keeps records of how many fires it and other agencies monitor instead of suppress. But ecologists understand the need for fire in the landscape. "Every time you put a fire out, you're just postponing it," fire ecologist Malcolm North said. "You just increase the actual fuel load that is out there, so when it does happen you get these massive megafire events."

WILDFIRE SAFETY TIPS

Human carelessness causes most wildfires. The US Department of the Interior's blog offers ten crucial tips on preventing wildfire. Many have to do with automotive safety.

- **Weather alerts and drought conditions should be noted and carefully considered. If it is windy, hot, and dry, don't do anything that involves fire, such as building a campfire or operating equipment that may produce sparks.**
- **Campfires should be built in open areas far from anything combustible. Build the fire on bare earth—not grass or leaves. Pile short pieces of wood in the open area. Never leave the fire unattended. Do not leave until you are certain the fire is out.**
- **Make certain that your campfire is cold when you leave. After you think it is extinguished, pour a pail of water on it, stir it up, pour another pail of water, and stir it a second time.**
- **Cars should not be driven over, or parked on, dry grass. Exhaust from a vehicle can reach 1,000°F (538°C) or more.**
- **Cars should be checked regularly. Malfunctioning equipment can cause sparks to discharge from the tailpipe.**

The Lions Fire: A Mind of Its Own

When lightning sparked a blaze at 8,000-foot-high (2,440 m) Lion Point in the Ansel Adams Wilderness south of Yosemite National Park in June 2018, district park ranger Denise Tolmie saw no reason to suppress it. The area was damp, cool, and remote. It abounded in trees that had been killed by insects or felled by the wind. Years of dried

- **Buckets, shovels, and fire extinguishers should be kept in cars in the event of a fire. Vehicles that will be driven in off-road locations are required to have a spark arrester, a device that prevents flammable emissions.**
- **Trailers should have tires, bearings, and axles checked regularly for safety.**
- **Any activity that produces sparks should never be done close to dry grasses or vegetation.**
- **All local, federal, state, and city regulations pertaining to fireworks must be followed. According to the Department of the Interior, over nineteen thousand fires are started by fireworks each year. Over nine thousand people receive serious injuries.**
- **Extreme care should be used when burning leaves, trash, or debris—especially when it's windy. Burning should be done close to a water source. Once out, the fire should be doused with water and stirred as in the case of a campfire.**

After it surged, the Lions Fire could be seen burning through the forest for miles.

leaves and undergrowth cluttered the ground. A good fire would clear the forest floor and reduce the fuel load as well as promote new growth. Instead of fighting the Lions Fire, crews monitored and contained it within natural boundaries, such as streams and boulders.

For several days, the fire crackled at low intensity, consuming dead branches and bushes just as anticipated. Then a sudden thunderstorm sent violent winds whipping into the area. Overnight the fire surged from 27 to 1,000 acres (11 to 405 ha). Unrestrained by natural boundaries, it expanded over weeks to almost 13,000 acres (5,260 ha). Smoke poured into the ski resort town of Mammoth Lakes, 7 miles (11 km) away. "This fire is doing a lot of things we didn't expect," Deb Schweizer, public affairs officer of Inyo National Forest, added. "It has pushed our hand. This fire has a mind of its own."

Responding to the growing crisis, the Forest Service launched full-scale suppression tactics. They flew in firefighters to combat the blaze. Helicopters dropped water. On October 7, 2018, almost four months after its initial reporting, the Lions Fire was contained. In the areas where it had burned, black, fertile ash had replaced the dried debris, a hopeful sign for a revitalized future.

Washburn and Oak Fires: What Made the Difference

Every fire is different, and every fire has something to teach us. For example, two fires with very different trajectories burned in the Sierra Nevada in July 2022. The first, the Washburn Fire, erupted on July 7 in Yosemite National Park near a road used by shuttle buses to transport visitors. Thick shrubbery lined the road. Park administrators worried that the fire could grow into an inferno. Over a dozen helicopters and sixteen hundred firefighters battled the blaze, which burned between July 7 and August 3. But the fire did not damage any buildings or a stand of giant sequoia trees in the nearby Mariposa Grove.

Two weeks after the Washburn Fire started, another fire broke out 17 miles (27 km) away and outside of the park, and it was a much different story. Fed by dense, withered vegetation, the Oak Fire grew rapidly and spawned an at least 20,000-foot-high (6,100 m) pyrocumulus cloud. By July 25, more than two thousand personnel worked to suppress the blaze with seventeen helicopters, 225 fire engines, twenty-three water tenders (specialized vehicles to supply fire engines with water), and fifty-eight bulldozers. Before firefighters contained the fire on August 10, more than 19,000 acres (7,690 ha) burned. More than one hundred homes were destroyed, and thousands were evacuated.

Why was the Oak Fire so much worse than the Washburn Fire? Although many factors played a role, the way each landscape had been tended made one of the biggest differences. A series of prescribed burns in 2017 had cleared out dried underbrush and small trees from the Mariposa Grove. On reaching the grove, the Washburn Fire encountered the area that had been burned, which slowed the wildfire and helped firefighters divert it around the iconic sequoia trees. Fuel reduction work that had been done along a nearby road in 2020 also made it safer for firefighters to confront the flames.

The Oak Fire burned quickly through untended dry, dense vegetation, but it slowed down when it encountered fire scars (scorched areas) from previous large fires and became easier to contain. According to Eric Knapp, a research ecologist with the Forest Service, prescribed burns are "the most effective tool" lessening the risk of fire. "You can be proactive or you can wait for a wildfire to hit with really bad fuels and have a different outcome," he explained. "And we all know we don't like that outcome."

Start with the Community

There is no one-method-fits-all approach for reducing fire risk. A state such as California with many ecosystems requires varied approaches. Small prescribed burns, mowing, and grazing work best in woodlands to purge overgrown vegetation. A dense forest may require more fire.

Communities situated in the wildland-urban interface, the region between urban and wild areas, pose the most critical challenge. Sometimes homes are built near wild landscapes of chaparral, tangled bushes, and shrubs. Then cutting back vegetation to create firebreaks seems to work best. Jon Keeley, a fire scientist with the US Geological Survey's Western Ecological Research Center in Sequoia and Kings Canyon National Parks, stresses the need to prioritize fuel reduction efforts. "Start with the community, and work outwards," he said. "Focus on where the real risks are."

Concentrating on reducing dry brush and chaparral close to neighborhoods may mean the difference between the devastation and preservation of homes. The La Tuna Fire in the Verdugo Mountains of Los Angeles County illustrates this. In the fall of 2018, high temperatures and fierce winds whipped the flames into what then mayor Eric Garcetti called the "largest fire in the history of Los Angeles."

Chaparral, such as that in California, is especially susceptible to fire during the summer when the weather is hot and dry.

Within hours, the flames encompassed thousands of acres. The freeway had to be closed in both directions, and hundreds of people were evacuated.

Almost fourteen hundred homes were endangered as the blaze advanced through the La Tuna Canyon. Some were as close as 200 feet (61 m) to the fire. But only five homes burned down. More than 99 percent escaped destruction.

The seemingly miraculous situation is the result of carefully maintained defensible spaces around the houses. Residents must clear a 100-foot (30.5 m) perimeter of flammable shrubs, twigs, and other possible combustible materials every spring. The city conducts annual inspections to ensure residents comply with the regulations. If homeowners do not comply, city or county workers complete the task for them, and the homeowners are charged a fee. In addition to this critical practice, strict building codes require the most updated fire safety measures in all new buildings or remodeled homes. The few homes that were destroyed were in isolated areas and had somehow missed the yearly inspection or lacked safeguards such as fire-resistant roofs.

INDIGENOUS PARTNERSHIPS

Recognizing the need for fire in the environment and concerned by the growing logging industry, many ecologists see hope in Indigenous peoples' traditional ecological knowledge. Eventually, this has led to some important partnerships between tribal nations and state and federal organizations. Preserving the environment goes hand in hand with honoring the culture and sacred traditions of Indigenous people. For example, Coast Miwok people work closely with the park staff of California's Muir Woods in research, education, revitalizing their cultural traditions, and maintaining sites that hold special meaning for them.

The Karuk, Yurok, and Hoopa Tribes of Northern California also seek cultural renewal in their relationships with federal agencies. "People have become disconnected with the land and fire," Robbins, a member of the Yurok Tribe, explained. "And they've forgotten . . . [or] perhaps they never knew who we [were] and who we're meant to be. . . . Fire has the ability to reestablish that connection."

Working with the Nature Conservancy, a nonprofit global environmental organization, and the Forest Service, the Karuk, Yurok, and Hoopa Tribes became members of the conservancy's prescribed fire training exchanges program. It sought people from diverse backgrounds to learn fire techniques and traditions from one another. The program aims to qualify more people to conduct prescribed burns at the federal, state, and private levels and to educate young people in fire culture. Tribal members who participate are eligible to help people conduct burns near their houses.

In 2015 leaders from the Karuk, Yurok, and Hoopa Tribes met with officials from the Nature Conservancy to discuss how Native Americans could strengthen existing fire systems. Their talks resulted in the creation of the Indigenous Peoples Burning Network to revive the fire legacy of past generations, to train people in both

New grass grows through freshly burned ground near Happy Camp, California. A member of the Indigenous Peoples Burning Network, the Karuk Tribe has used fire to help maintain the landscape in that region for millennia.

federal requirements and the cultural values of controlled burning, and to teach fire knowledge to young people.

Since it was founded in 2015, the network has welcomed people from New Mexico pueblos; the Leech Lake Band of Ojibwe in Minnesota; the Klamath Tribes in Oregon, which include the Klamath, the Modoc, and the Yahooskin-Paiute; and the Alabama-Coushatta Tribe of Texas. The Indigenous leadership of the network and its reliance on traditional fire culture make it unique among fire-managing organizations.

We Have a Choice

Although no fire event—whether prescribed or natural—is completely without risk, responsible forest and fire management greatly lessens the threat to human communities and minimizes the chance that future fires will rage out of control. A series of fires in 2012 prompted retired Forest Service manager Bob Mutch to present stark alternatives. "We have a choice on how we receive the inevitable smoke from Montana's fires," he wrote, "in smaller, regular doses over time, the result of free-burning fires in wilderness and sound forest management practices outside wilderness, or in supersized doses from megafires that are the result of fire exclusion, unnatural fuel accumulations, and a changing climate."

CONCLUSION

IN 2022, FOUR YEARS AFTER THE DESTRUCTION OF PARADISE, California, the town's restoration continued. Debris and hazardous waste had been removed from private and public property. A park and a scenic road that is popular with cyclists had reopened. As of November 2022, more than fourteen hundred homes had been rebuilt, and almost ten thousand people lived in the growing town.

"Nobody who was here gave up," said Gwen Nordgren, president of Paradise Lutheran Church. "There's a spirit in this town that was here before the fire, and that's here now, and it never went away."

The town has a new look thanks to a number of noncombustible homes that have replaced the destroyed buildings. One such house belongs to Mike Petersen, who manages a hardware store that escaped destruction but whose house did not. The Q Cabins into which residents such as Petersen have moved take after round-roofed, metal buildings first built in World War II. According to Vern Sneed, the owner of Design Horizons, which makes Q Cabin kit homes, the

Paradise in 2023. Residents have continued to revitalize the town following the Camp Fire.

siding, sheathing, and structure are made of material that does not burn. The corrugated metal roof and the windows have no spots where a stray ember could enter the home, which is the most common way house fires start. With more and more homes being built in the wildland-urban interface, Sneed believes that "noncombustible housing is the future."

The lessons learned from the destruction of Paradise can significantly motivate other communities to prepare for possible catastrophe. The town's fate prompted a statewide initiative, Listos California, to help residents of areas especially susceptible to natural disasters such as wildfires, earthquakes, or floods. Listos means "ready" in Spanish, and the program promises "resources to ready immigrant and farmworker communities in their native languages." The program provides the information and help needed to prepare for, withstand, and recover from a disaster. Between 2019 and 2021, more than four million people with disabilities, language barriers, low-income status, or other circumstances that make them particularly vulnerable to disaster received information from Listos California.

Many Heroes

Many people have a role to play in managing fire—hotshots and ground crews, aerial crews and smoke jumpers, ecologists and rangers who carefully ignite prescribed burns after studying all the conditions, Indigenous fire practitioners whose cultural burns benefit the ecology and promote biodiversity, and more. Campers and hikers do their part by following the safety rules for campfires and vehicles. Homeowners, especially those in high-risk fire zones, protect their property by following building codes, removing dry brush, and creating defensive spaces around their homes.

"Fire is part of nature," said John Waconda, a member of the Isleta Pueblo and the Indigenous Partnerships Program director with the Nature Conservancy. "It's just like the rain, the sunrise each day. It's a natural occurrence, a part of nature necessary to complete lifecycles of different plants and animals."

Necessary to humans too, fire continues to fascinate, sustain, and frighten us. Climate change and the legacy of a century of fire suppression challenge our relationship with fire. There will always be megafires that devour acres of land, threaten communities, and resist attempts to contain them. But fire isn't always an opponent. With the right attitudes, practices, and protective measures, fire is often an ally and an indispensable tool in preserving flourishing and diverse ecosystems.

"Fire is part of nature. It's just like the rain, the sunrise each day. It's a natural occurance . . . necessary to complete lifecycles of different plants and animals."

TIMELINE

ca. 3000s BCE Indigenous people use fire to shape the land to benefit their livelihood and culture.

ca. 1800s CE Westward expansion pushes Native peoples off their ancestral lands. Many settlers were suspicious of Native Americans' use of fire and wanted it outlawed.

1871 The Great Chicago Fire erupts on October 8.

The Peshtigo Fire kills more than fifteen hundred people, making it the deadliest fire in American history.

1905 The Forest Service is established on February 1.

1910 The Big Blowup burns more than 3 million acres (1.2 million ha) and kills eighty-five people on August 20 to 21.

Gifford Pinchot convinces Congress to provide more money to the Forest Service to suppress wildfire.

1935 The Fire Service's 10 a.m. policy specifies that all wildfires must be controlled by 10 a.m. the morning after they are reported.

1940 The first smoke jumpers parachute into a remote portion of the Nez Perce National Forest in Idaho.

1944 Smokey Bear becomes the mascot of the Forest Service's campaign to prevent wildfires.

1960s Prescribed burns slowly resume in the United States.

1963 The Leopold Report calls for the reintroduction of fire into the American landscape.

1968	The National Park Service adopts a new policy acknowledging the need for prescribed burns.
	Park rangers ignite a controlled burn in Sequoia and Kings Canyon National Parks.
2000s	Heat waves, droughts, and high winds caused by climate change continue to lengthen the fire season and increase the intensity of wildfires.
2007	The Swinomish become the first North American Indigenous tribe to issue a climate proclamation. A climate action plan follows three years later.
2015	The Indigenous Peoples Burning Network is established.
2020	The first robotic firefighting vehicle in the United States debuts in Los Angeles.
2022	The United Nations Environment Programme issues a report that draws a distinction between destructive wildfires and landscape fires that may benefit the environment.
2023	The United Nations acknowledges the importance of Indigenous people's knowledge and insight in confronting the climate crisis.

GLOSSARY

aerial fire suppression: the use of aircraft to contain a wildfire

carbon capture: capturing CO_2 produced by burning fossil fuels and storing it so that it cannot enter the atmosphere and contribute to climate change

climate change: shifts in the earth's temperatures and weather patterns. They can be due to natural causes such as solar activity or to human activity such as the emission of greenhouse gases by the burning of fossil fuels.

climate migrant: someone who voluntarily moves to another place because of a sudden or gradual change in climate

combustion: when a substance (fuel) combines with oxygen in the atmosphere to produce heat and light

cultural burns: carefully controlled fires set by Indigenous people to shape the landscape in ways that support their livelihood and culture

ecological succession: the gradual replacement of plants over time in an environment by other species

ecosystem: a geographic area in which plants, animals, and other organisms interact with one another and the environment

enhanced weathering: a technology to remove CO_2 from the atmosphere by spreading crushed rock on land or the ocean to accelerate the natural production of bicarbonate

firebreak: a natural or human-made barrier intended to slow or stop a moving fire

fire ecology: a branch of ecology that deals with wildfire and its relationship to the ecosystem

fire regime: the relationship between a specific locale and the kind of fire it is likely to encounter on a regular basis. Frequency, intensity, seasonality, and spread determine an ecosystem's fire regime.

fire retardant: a chemical substance used to slow down or stop a fire or reduce its intensity

fire tornado: a rapidly spinning vortex of flame and smoke rising above an intense fire; also called a firenado

fire triangle: the three elements required to ignite a fire—fuel, oxygen, and heat

fire whirl: a small twister, usually composed of flame and ash, induced by a fire

fossil fuel: a material containing hydrocarbon that is formed from the remains of prehistoric plants and animals and is extracted from the earth to be used as fuel

germinate: to cause to sprout or develop

greenhouse effect: the warming of the earth's atmosphere caused by the accumulation of CO_2 in the atmosphere from the burning of fossil fuels

high-intensity fire: a hard-to-suppress, extreme fire caused by hot, dry, windy conditions, an abundance of fuel, and often a steep terrain

hotshot: a member of a team of highly trained, elite firefighters that are sent to suppress wildland fires across the country

hydrocarbon: a substance made only of hydrogen and carbon, such as coal or petroleum

ignition point: the lowest temperature at which a combustible material is able to catch fire and burn without an external flame or ignition source

Industrial Revolution: the transition in 1760 to 1840 from an agricultural to an industrial economy characterized by the burning of fossil fuels to power engines and machines

invasive species: plants, animals, or microorganisms that spread beyond their natural habitat and have the potential to harm species native to the expanded area

keystone species: a species necessary to the well-being or even the existence of an ecosystem

megafire: an increasingly frequent phenomenon defined by the US Interagency Fire Center as a fire that burns more than 100,000 acres (40,500 ha) of land

piloted ignition temperature: the amount of heat needed for a specific substance to ignite in the presence of a spark

prescribed burn: an intentionally set, carefully controlled fire to remove dried underbrush and lessen the impact of a future fire

pyrocumulonimbus: anvil-shaped thunder clouds that spawn lightning and high winds. Generally shortened to pyroCb, they form above a source of heat such as a wildfire or a volcanic eruption.

pyrocumulus: a dense fire cloud formed when water vapor condenses on particles of ash in the smoke from a wildfire

pyrophilic plant: a vegetation that cannot reproduce without fire

pyrophyte: a plant that has evolved to protect itself from fire in ways that promote the survival of its species. Passive pyrophytes endure fire but do not help spread it. Active pyrophytes have developed in ways that promote the spread of fire.

smoke jumper: a firefighter who parachutes from a plane to the site of a wildfire

snag: a standing dead tree

unpiloted ignition temperature: the temperature at which a specific substance can catch fire without a spark

wildland-urban interface: a region where a natural environment such as the wilderness meets an environment that humans built or developed. These areas face a higher risk of intense wildfires.

zombie fire: a fire occurring in northern latitudes that smolder underground for the winter and reemerge in the spring; also called overwintering or holdover fire

SOURCE NOTES

5–6 "There was just . . . it was developing.": *Fire in Paradise*, transcript of video, *Frontline*, updated July 6, 2021, https://www.pbs.org/wgbh/frontline/documentary/fire-in-paradise/transcript.

6 "Are we gonna die?": Rong-Gong Lin II and Maria L. La Ganga, "They Thought They'd Die Trapped in a Parking Lot. How 150 Survivors of California's Deadliest Fire Made It out Alive," *Los Angeles Times*, December 2, 2018, https://www.latimes.com/local/lanow/la-me-ln-paradise-survivors-20181202-htmlstory.html.

12 "scenery and wildlife . . . sea of green.": Monica G. Turner, "30 Years Later: Yellowstone's 1988 Fires Revealed Resilience of Forests," Treesource, September 3, 2018, https://treesource.org/news/lands/yellowstone-fires/.

13 "A forest in . . . area encourages growth.": Gigi Ragland, "Public Lands Transformed: Inside Parks' Wildfire Recovery," *Sierra*, July 14, 2021, https://www.sierraclub.org/sierra/public-lands-transformed-inside-parks-wildfire-recovery.

18 "Fire is what . . . it changes everything.": Brianna Randall, "The Great Plains Prairie Needs Fire to Survive. These Ranchers Are Bringing It Back," *National Geographic*, May 13, 2021, https://www.nationalgeographic.com/environment/article/great-plains-prairie-needs-fire-to-survive-these-ranchers-are-bringing-it-back.

31, 33 "Fire itself is . . . science currently understands.": Bill Tripp, "Our Land Was Taken. But We Still Hold the Knowledge of How to Stop Mega-Fires," *Guardian* (US edition), September 16, 2020, https://www.theguardian.com/commentisfree/2020/sep/16/california-wildfires-cultural-burns-indigenous-people.

33 "Indigenous people had . . . using cultural burns.": Andrew Avitt, "Tribal and Indigenous Fire Tradition," US Forest Service, November 16, 2021, https://www.fs.usda.gov/features/tribal-and-indigenous-heritage.

35 "As aboriginal people . . . care of you.": Mike Cherney, "To Prevent Huge Wildfires, Australia Leans More on Indigenous Experience," *Wall Street Journal*, February 16, 2023, https://www.wsj.com/articles/to-prevent-huge-wildfires-australia-leans-more-on-indigenous-wisdom-77d2ca0d.

36 "Land needs fire.": Kylie Stevenson, "How Australia's Aboriginal People Fight Fire—with Fire," *National Geographic*, March 24, 2023, https://www.nationalgeographic.com/magazine/article/how-australias-aboriginal-people-fight-fire-with-fire-feature.

37 "for service to . . . of rock art": "Honors List," Australian Government Department of the Prime Minister and Cabinet, accessed June 29, 2023, https://honours.pmc.gov.au/honours/awards/1055949.

43 "the deadliest fire in American history": Tom Hultquist, "The Great Midwest Wildfires of 1871," National Weather Service, accessed June 29, 2023, https://www.weather.gov/grb/peshtigofire2.

43 "You are engaged . . . to the work.": "The Big Burn," *American Experience*, aired September 7, 2022, https://www.pbs.org/wgbh/americanexperience/films/burn/#transcript.

44 "Everyone lived with . . . from their houses.": "Prescribed Burning Is a Tradition for Floridians," St. Johns River Water Management District, February 9, 2023, https://www.sjrwmd.com/streamlines/prescribed-burning-is-a-tradition-for-floridians.

45 "The whole world . . . of the world.": "Blazing Battles: The 1910 Fire and Its Legacy," *Your National Forests*, accessed June 29, 2023, https://www.nationalforests.org/our-forests/your-national-forests-magazine/blazing-battles-the-1910-fire-and-its-legacy.

46 "Come on! Come on! Follow me.": "The Big Burn," *American Experience*.

48 "represent a vignette . . . the white man.": Stephen J. Pyne, "Vignettes of Primitive America: The Leopold Report and Fire Policy." *Forest History Today* (Spring 2017): 12.

49 "depressing . . . natural ground fires.": Pyne, 13.

49 "Over my dead body!": Bruce M. Kilgore, "Origin and History of Wildland Fire Use in the U.S. National Park System," *George Wright Forum* 24, no. 3 (2007), http://www.georgewright.org/243kilgore.pdf, 101.

49 "the presence or . . . for natural fire.": Kilgore, 102.

50 "Forest Fires Aid . . . Their Secret Weapon": "About the Campaign," Smokey Bear, accessed June 29, 2023, https://smokeybear.com/en/smokeys-history/about-the-campaign.

50 "Only you can prevent forest fires.": Lyndsie Bourgon, "A Brief History of Smokey Bear, the Forest Service's Legendary Mascot," *Smithsonian*, July 2019, https://www.smithsonianmag.com/history/brief-history-smokey-bear-180972549.

50 "Only you can . . . his message is.": Bourgon.

51 "No one can . . . fires. Be ready.": Brian Faler, "Group's Fire Mascot Seeks to Get on Top of Old Smokey," *Washington Post*, August 23, 2002, https://www.washingtonpost.com/archive/politics/2002/08/23/groups-fire-mascot-seeks-to-get-on-top-of-old-smokey/cb7f1f04-21b8-4a63-bda7-ad8c72953e88.

51 "But Reddy has . . . understands fire ecology.": Editors of *E Magazine*, "Smokey Bear's Squirrelly Sister," *Environmental Magazine*, July 20, 2004, https://emagazine.com/smokey-bears-squirrelly-sister.

54 "The beauty of . . . there as well.": Aaron Derr, "Philmont Continues to Navigate Fire Safety as Season Begins as Scheduled," *Scouting*, June 10, 2022, https://blog.scoutingmagazine.org/2022/06/10/philmont-continues-to-navigate-fire-safety-summer-season-begins-as-scheduled.

55 "eco-disaster[s]": Chad Hanson, *Smokescreen: Debunking Wildfire Myths to Save Our Forests and Our Climate* (Lexington: University Press of Kentucky, 2010), 28.

58 "Climate change is . . . see until 2080.": Andrew Moore, "Climate Change Is Making Wildfires Worse—Here's How," College of Natural Resources News, North Carolina State University, August 29, 2022, https://cnr.ncsu.edu/news/2022/08/climate-change-wildfires-explained.

59 "The massive winds . . . on the islands.": Christopher Flavelle and Manuela Andreoni, "How Climate Change Turned Lush Hawaii into a Tinderbox," *New York Times*, updated August 14, 2023, https://www.nytimes.com/2023/08/10/climate/hawaii-fires-climate-change.html.

59 "a very powerful . . . through this crisis": Joe Biden, "Remarks by President Biden Paying Respects to the Lives Lost in Maui and Reaffirming His Commitment to Supporting Residents," transcript of speech given in Lahaina, Hawaii, August 21, 2023, https://www.whitehouse.gov/briefing-room/speeches-remarks/2023/08/21/remarks-by-president-biden-paying-respects-to-the-lives-lost-in-maui-and-reaffirming-his-commitment-to-supporting-residents.

61 "remind us that . . . accelerates climate change.": Isabella Kaminski, "Did Climate Change Cause Canada's Wildfires?," BBC, June 12, 2023, https://www.bbc.com/future/article/20230612-did-climate-change-cause-canadas-wildfires.

63 "An atmosphere of . . . a high temperature.": John Schwartz, "Overlooked No More: Eunice Foote, Climate Scientist Lost to History," *New York Times*, updated April 27, 2020, https://www.nytimes.com/2020/04/21/obituaries/eunice-foote-overlooked.html.

66 "resources to burn . . . conditions, and ignitions": Michael Kodas, *Megafire: The Race to Extinguish a Deadly Epidemic of Flame* (Boston: Houghton Mifflin Harcourt, 2017), 153.

67 "integrated wildfire management . . . response, and recovery": United Nations Environment Programme, *Spreading Like Wildfire: The Rising Threat of Extraordinary Landscape Fires* (Nairobi, Kenya: United Nations Environment Programme, 2022), 12.

68 "Increases and decreases . . . makes it healthy.": Kodas, 153.

69 "It's getting warmer . . . [severely burned] areas.": Chelsea Harvey, "Fires Doubled Australia's Carbon Emissions – Ecosystems May Never Soak It Back Up," *Scientific American*, January 11, 2022, https://www.scientificamerican.com/article/fires-doubled-australias-carbon-emissions-ecosystems-may-never-soak-it-back-up/.

70 "We need to . . . of carbon removal.": Renee Cho, "Can Removing Carbon from the Atmosphere Save Us from Climate Catastrophe?," Columbia Climate School, November 27, 2018, https://news.climate.columbia.edu/2018/11/27/carbon-dioxide-removal-climate-change/.

71 "Forests respond within . . . of mineral ash.": Hanson, 86.

72 "Oil is the . . . of Mother Earth.": Geraldine Patrick Encina and Karl Burkart, "Biodiversity Must Be at the Heart of the Global Financial System," One Earth, May 3, 2023, https://www.oneearth.org/biodiversity-must-be-at-the-heart-of-the-global-financial-system.

72 "have unique connections . . . and most severely.": Nicola Jones, "How Native Tribes Are Taking the Lead on Planning for Climate Change," Yale Environment 360, Yale University, February 11, 2020, https://e360.yale.edu/features/how-native-tribes-are-taking-the-lead-on-planning-for-climate-change.

73 "What we have . . . to the challenge.": "Swinomish Climate Change Initiative Climate Adaption Action Plan," Swinomish Indian Tribal Community, October 2010, https://swinomish-nsn.gov/media/54202/swin_cr_2010_01_ccadaptationplan.pdf.

75 "fire-breathing dragon of clouds": Katharine Gammon, "'Fire-Breathing Dragon Clouds': A Wildfire-Fueled Phenomenon Explained," *Guardian* (US edition), August 6, 2022, https://www.theguardian.com/world/2022/aug/05/pyrocumulonimbus-clouds-wildfire-mckinney-fire.

78 "The term catastrophic . . . no scientific credibility.": Jimmy Tobias, "Stop with the 'Catastrophic Wildfire' Scare Tactics," *Pacific Standard*, August 15, 2017, https://psmag.com/environment/a-catastrophic-scare-tactic.

79 "Fire tornadoes are . . . a regular tornado.": Nick Mott, "Scientists Are Learning More about Fire Tornadoes, the Spinning Funnels of Flame," National Public Radio, August 23, 2021, https://www.npr.org/2021/08/23/1029638870/fire-tornadoes-scientists-funnels-flames.

81 "Hopefully we can . . . of the way.": Ken Brunhuber, "Creating a Fire Tornado: Montana Lab Seeks to Unlock the Mysteries of Wildfire," CBC News, April 22, 2019, https://www.cbc.ca/news/world/wildfire-lab-fire-research-1.5102583.

84 "Firefighting is not . . . who they were.": Shaun McKinnon, "How Joe Biden's Last Eulogy in Arizona Helped 19 Families Grieve," AZ Central, updated August 27, 2018, https://www.azcentral.com/story/news/politics/arizona/2018/08/27/joe-biden-delivered-eulogy-granite-mountain-hotshots-john-mccain/1111660002.

86 “the best and . . . I’ve ever had”: “The History of Hotshot Firefighters,” National Fire Fighter Corp., July 1, 2015, https://www.nationalfirefighter.com/blogihq/The-History-of-Hotshot-Firefighters.

87 “I wanted to . . . safer out there?”: Brendan McDonough, “How We Can Make Wildland Firefighting Safer,” *Outside*, June 16, 2016, https://www.outsideonline.com/outdoor-adventure/exploration-survival/how-we-can-make-wildland-firefighting-safer.

87 “living for the next 120 seconds”: McDonough.

87 “The more resources . . . is for everyone.”: McDonough.

91 “It is the . . . them under control.”: Frontline Wildfire Defense, “Aerial Firefighters & Fire Fighting: Dangerous . . . but Effective?,” Frontline Wildfire Defense, accessed June 29, 2023, https://www.frontlinewildfire.com/wildfire-news-and-resources/aerial-wildfire-fighting-how-effective-is-it/.

93–94 “Actual firefighters . . . a lot easier.”: Kodas, 217.

94 “There’s no scientific . . . it doesn’t work.”: Alex Wigglesworth, “Aerial Fire Retardant Drops Are Attacked as Ineffective and Environmentally Harmful,” *Los Angeles Times*, updated March 29, 2023, https://www.latimes.com/california/story/2023-03-29/u-s-forest-service-defends-use-of-pink-wildfire-retardant.

97 “[Firefighters’] respiratory demands . . . your cognitive abilities.”: Jes Burns, “Not Enough Is Known about Smoke’s Effect on Wildland Firefighters’ Health,” OPB, May 29, 2019, https://www.opb.org/news/article/health-wildland-firefighters-smoke-breathing-lungs.

97 “Firefighter and public . . . to be safer.”: Amy B. Wang, “Has Yarnell Hill Fire Changed Way Crews Fight Fires?,” AZ Central, last updated June 25, 2014, https://www.azcentral.com/story/news/arizona/2014/06/25/yarnell-hill-arizona-wildfire-crews/11344517.

98 “Flying over that . . . in many cases.”: “Hickenlooper: Devastation from Flames ‘Sobering,’” CBS Colorado, March 29, 2012, https://www.cbsnews.com/colorado/news/gov-hickenlooper-devastation-from-flames-sobering.

100 “If we made . . . any of those?”: Associated Press, “Governor Hickenlooper Takes Helicopter Tour of Wildfire,” 9 News Denver, March 29, 2012, https://www.9news.com/article/news/local/politics/governor-hickenlooper-takes-helicopter-tour-of-wildfire/73-333813576.

101 “We conduct an . . . can always improve.”: “From the Chief’s Desk: Reviewing Our Prescribed Fire Program,” USDA Forest Service, May 20, 2022, https://www.fs.usda.gov/inside-fs/leadership/chiefs-desk-reviewing-our-prescribed-fire-program.

102 “the equivalent of a flight simulator”: Rodman Linn and J. Kevin Hiers, “Fighting Wildfires with Computer Models,” *Scientific American*, August 27, 2019, https://blogs.scientificamerican.com/observations/fighting-wildfires-with-computer-models.

103 “to improve the . . . for catastrophic wildfires.”: “From the Chief’s,” USDA.

103 “It’s pretty much . . . Forest Service jurisdictions.”: Alex Wigglesworth, “Forest Service Resumes Prescribed Fire Program, but Some Fear New Rules Will Delay Projects,” *Los Angeles Times*, September 13, 2022, https://www.latimes.com/california/story/2022-09-13/forest-service-resumes-prescribed-burning.

103 “We need prescribed . . . the short run.”: Wigglesworth.

104 “Every time you . . . massive megafire events.”: Nathan Rott, “Fire Ecologists Say More Fires Should Be Left to Burn. So Why Aren’t They?,” *All Things Considered*, National Public Radio, September 27, 2018, https://www.npr.org/2018/09/27/649649316/fire-ecologists-say-more-fires-should-be-left-to-burn-so-why-arent-they.

106 “This fire is . . . of its own.”: Lisa Krieger, “Some Experts Question CA Wildfire Strategy,” *Firehouse Magazine*, September 19, 2018, https://www.firehouse.com/operations-training/wildland/news/21023220/experts-question-success-of-ca-wildfire-strategy-firefighters.

108 “the most effective . . . like that outcome.”: Caroline Mimbs Nyce, “Those Sequoias Didn’t Just Get Lucky,” *Atlantic*, July 14, 2022, https://www.theatlantic.com/ideas/archive/2022/07/yosemites-washburn-fire-sequoias/670520.

108 "Start with the . . . real risks are.": Krieger.

108 "largest fire in . . . of Los Angeles": Safia Samee Ali, "La Tuna Fire in Los Angeles Grows to Thousands of Acres, Largest Brush Fire in City History," NBC News, September 2, 2017, https://www.nbcnews.com/news/us-news/la-tuna-fire-los-angeles-grows-thousands-acres-largest-brush-n798326.

110 "People have become . . . reestablish that connection.": Page Buono, "Quiet Fire," *Nature Conservancy*, November 2, 2020, https://www.nature.org/en-us/magazine/magazine-articles/indigenous-controlled-burns-california.

112 "We have a . . . a changing climate.": Kodas, 138.

113 "Nobody who was . . . never went away.": John Goodwin, "After the Camp Fire: Rebuilding Paradise," CBS News, May 29, 2022, https://www.cbsnews.com/news/after-the-camp-fire-rebuilding-paradise-constructing-for-wildfires.

114 "noncombustible housing is the future": Goodwin.

114 "resources to ready . . . their native languages": "Home," Listos California, accessed June 29, 2023, https://www.listoscalifornia.org.

115 "Fire is part . . . plants and animals.": Andrew Avitt, "Tribal and Indigenous Fire Tradition," US Forest Service, November 16, 2021, https://www.fs.usda.gov/features/tribal-and-indigenous-heritage.

SELECTED BIBLIOGRAPHY

"Aerial Firefighters & Fire Fighting: Dangerous . . . but Effective?" Frontline Wildfire Defense. Accessed June 29, 2023. https://www.frontlinewildfire.com/wildfire-news-and-resources/aerial-wildfire-fighting-how-effective-is-it/.

Ali, Safia Samee. "La Tuna Fire in Los Angeles Grows to Thousands of Acres, 'Largest' Brush Fire in City History." NBC News, September 2, 2017. https://www.nbcnews.com/news/us-news/la-tuna-fire-los-angeles-grows-thousands-acres-largest-brush-n798326.

"Annual 2022 Wildfires Report." National Centers for Environmental Information, National Oceanic and Atmospheric Association, January 2023. https://www.ncei.noaa.gov/access/monitoring/monthly-report/fire/202213.

Associated Press. "Governor Hickenlooper Takes Helicopter Tour of Wildfire." 9 News Denver, March 29, 2012. https://www.9news.com/article/news/local/politics/governor-hickenlooper-takes-helicopter-tour-of-wildfire/73-333813576.

Avitt, Andrew. "Tribal and Indigenous Fire Tradition." US Forest Service, November 16, 2021. https://www.fs.usda.gov/features/tribal-and-indigenous-heritage.

"The Big Burn." *American Experience.* Aired September 7, 2022. https://www.pbs.org/wgbh/americanexperience/films/burn/#transcript.

"Blazing Battles: The 1910 Fire and Its Legacy." *Your National Forests,* National Forest Service. Accessed June 29, 2023. https://www.nationalforests.org/our-forests/your-national-forests-magazine/blazing-battles-the-1910-fire-and-its-legacy.

Boghani, Priyanka. "Camp Fire: By the Numbers." *Frontline*, October 29, 2019. https://www.pbs.org/wgbh/frontline/article/camp-fire-by-the-numbers/.

Borunda, Alejandra. "Zombie Fires in the Arctic Are Linked to Climate Change." *National Geographic*, May 19, 2021. https://www.nationalgeographic.com/environment/article/zombie-fires-in-the-arctic-are-linked-to-climate-change.

Braxton Little, Jane. "Firefighting Robots Go Autonomous." *Scientific American*, October 29, 2021. https://www.scientificamerican.com/article/firefighting-robots-go-autonomous.

Brunhuber, Ken. "Creating a Fire Tornado: Montana Lab Seeks to Unlock the Mysteries of Wildfire." CBC, April 22, 2019. https://www.cbc.ca/news/world/wildfire-lab-fire-research-1.5102583.

Buono, Page. "Quiet Fire." *Nature*, November 2, 2020. https://www.nature.org/en-us/magazine/magazine-articles/indigenous-controlled-burns-california.

Byrne, Brendan, J. Liu, M. Lee, Y. Yin, K. W. Bowman, K. Miyazaki, A. J. Norton, et al. "The Carbon Cycle of Southeast Australia during 2019–2020: Drought, Fires, and Subsequent Recovery." *AGU Advances* (December 2021). http://dx.doi.org/10.31223/X5PP6S.

Cappucci, Matthew. "California's Carr Fire Spawned a True Fire Tornado." ScienceNewsExplores, November 14, 2018. https://www.snexplores.org/article/californias-carr-fire-spawned-true-fire-tornado.

Cherney, Mark. "To Prevent Huge Wildfires, Australia Leans More on Indigenous Experience." *Wall Street Journal*, February 16, 2023. https://www.wsj.com/articles/to-prevent-huge-wildfires-australia-leans-more-on-indigenous-wisdom-77d2ca0d.

Cho, Renee. "Can Removing Carbon from the Atmosphere Save Us from Climate Catastrophe?" Columbia Climate School, November 27, 2018. https://news.climate.columbia.edu/2018/11/27/carbon-dioxide-removal-climate-change.

Chung, Christine. "Wildfire in Yosemite National Park Imperils Century-Old Trees." *New York Times*, July 10, 2022. https://www.nytimes.com/2022/07/10/us/washburn-fire-yosemite.html.

Derr, Aaron. "Philmont Continues to Navigate Fire Safety as Season Begins as Scheduled." *Scouting*, June 10, 2022. https://blog.scoutingmagazine.org/2022/06/10/philmont-continues-to-navigate-fire-safety-summer-season-begins-as-scheduled.

Dickman, Kyle. "What We Learned from the Yarnell Hill Fire Deaths." *Outside*. Updated May 12, 2022. https://www.outsideonline.com/outdoor-adventure/environment/what-we-learned-yarnell-hill-fire.

Dorman, Jon. "Peshtigo Fire: The Deadliest Wildfire in U.S. History." Fire Rescue 1, August 1, 2022. https://www.firerescue1.com/firefighting-history/articles/peshtigo-fire-the-deadliest-wildfire-in-us-history-Xe6TtkZVNuTix48C/.

Dorsch, Jim. "What Are the Eight Main Ecosystems?" Sciencing, November 22, 2019. https://sciencing.com/what-are-the-eight-main-ecosystems-12352395.html.

"The Ecological Importance of Forest Fires." Green Tumble, April 20, 2016. https://greentumble.com/the-ecological-importance-of-forest-fires.

Fisher, Richard. "Canada Wildfires: Will They Change How People Think about Climate Change?" BBC, June 8, 2023. https://www.bbc.com/future/article/20230608-canada-wildfires-will-they-change-climate-attitudes-on-us-east-coast.

"From the Chief's Desk: Reviewing Our Prescribed Fire Program." USDA Forest Service, May 20, 2022. https://www.fs.usda.gov/inside-fs/leadership/chiefs-desk-reviewing-our-prescribed-fire-program.

Fuller, Thomas. "California's Largest Wildfire Slows after Exploding near Yosemite." *New York Times*, July 25, 2022. https://www.nytimes.com/2022/07/25/us/oak-fire-yosemite-california.html.

Gillis, Justin. "Let Forest Fires Burn? What the Black-Backed Woodpecker Knows." *New York Times*, August 6, 2017. https://www.nytimes.com/2017/08/06/science/let-forest-fires-burn-what-the-black-backed-woodpecker-knows.html.

Giuliana-Hoffman, Francesca. "The First Firefighting Robot in America Is Here—and It Has Already Helped Fight a Major Fire in Los Angeles." CNN. Updated October 21, 2020. https://www.cnn.com/2020/10/21/business/first-firefighting-robot-in-america-lafd-trnd/index.html.

Glick, Daniel. "The Perfect Firestorm." *Audubon*, July–August 2011. https://www.audubon.org/magazine/july-august-2011/the-perfect-firestorm.

Glicksman, Eve. "Send in the Robots: A Look into the Future of Firefighting." Leaps.org, April 18, 2023. https://leaps.org/drone-with-camera.

"Habitat Management and Fact Sheet: Prescribed Burning." Indiana Division of Fish and Wildlife, Indiana Department of Natural Resources, March 2005. https://www.in.gov/dnr/fish-and-wildlife/files/HMFSPrescribedBurn.pdf.

Hancock, David. "Fire Money: How Indigenous Land Management Is Transforming Arnhem Land." *Guardian* (Australian edition). May 23, 2021. https://www.theguardian.com/australia-news/2021/may/24/fire-money-how-indigenous-land-management-is-transforming-arnhem-land.

Hanson, Chad. *Smokescreen: Debunking Wildfire Myths to Save Our Forests and Our Climate*. Lexington: University Press of Kentucky, 2010.

Harris, Tom. "How Fire Works," HowStuffWorks. Accessed June 29, 2023. https://science.howstuffworks.com/environmental/earth/geophysics/fire.htm/printable.

Harvey, Chelsea. "Fires Doubled Australia's Carbon Emissions—Ecosystems May Never Soak It Back Up." *Scientific American*, January 11, 2022. https://www.scientificamerican.com/article/fires-doubled-australias-carbon-emissions-ecosystems-may-never-soak-it-back-up/.

"Hickenlooper: Devastation from Flames 'Sobering.'" CBS Colorado, March 29, 2012. https://www.cbsnews.com/colorado/news/gov-hickenlooper-devastation-from-flames-sobering.

"How Indigenous Peoples Enrich Climate Action." United Nations Climate Change, August 9, 2022. https://unfccc.int/news/how-indigenous-peoples-enrich-climate-action?gclid=CjwKCAjwge2iBhBBEiwAfXDBR8LtJ01cikOJgd9WImKsXc2KfbaMtOEC5tTBtQnWdAOinvpgFzoAHxoCRsYQAvD_BwE.

"How Wildfires Impact Wildlife and Their Habitats." *PBS News Weekend*, October 23, 2021. https://www.pbs.org/newshour/science/explainer-how-wildfires-impact-wildlife-their-habitat.

"Huge Forest Fires Don't Cause Living Trees to Release Much Carbon, OSU Research Shows." Oregon State University, March 14, 2022. https://today.oregonstate.edu/news/huge-forest-fires-don't-cause-living-trees-release-much-carbon-osu-research-shows.

Hultquist, Tom. "The Great Midwest Wildfires of 1871." National Weather Service. Accessed June 29, 2023. https://www.weather.gov/grb/peshtigofire2.

Humphries, Alexandra. "Australia's Black Summer Bushfires Were Catastrophic Enough. Now Scientists Say They Caused a 'Deep, Long-Lived' Hole in the Ozone Layer." Australian Broadcasting Corporation. Updated August 26, 2022. https://www.abc.net.au/news/2022-08-26/black-summer-bushfires-caused-ozone-hole/101376644.

"Indigenous Peoples' Burning Network." Conservation Gateway, Nature Conservancy. Accessed June 29, 2023. https://conservationgateway.org/ConservationPractices/FireLandscapes/Pages/IPBN.aspx.

"Indigenous People's Knowledge, Insight Needed to Address Global Climate Crisis, Speakers Stress, as Permanent Forum Opens Session." United Nations, April 17, 2023. https://press.un.org/en/2023/hr5476.doc.htm.

"Influence of Fire on Human Evolution." Adventure Service. Updated September 26, 2023. https://www.theadventureservice.com/post/influence-of-fire-on-human-evolution.

Jones, Nicola. "How Native Tribes Are Taking the Lead on Planning for Climate Change." Yale Environment 360, February 11, 2020. https://e360.yale.edu/features/how-native-tribes-are-taking-the-lead-on-planning-for-climate-change.

Kilgore, Bruce M. "Wildland Fire History—The History of National Park Service Fire Policy." National Park Service. Accessed June 29, 2023. https://www.nps.gov/articles/the-history-of-national-park-service-fire-policy.htm.

Kimmerer, Robin Wall, and Frank Kanawha Lake. "The Role of Indigenous Burning in Land Management." *Journal of Forestry* (November 2001): 36–41.

Kodas, Michael. *Megafire: The Race to Extinguish a Deadly Epidemic of Flame*. Boston: Houghton Mifflin Harcourt, 2017.

Krieger, Lisa M. "Some Experts Question CA Wildfire Strategy." *Firehouse Magazine*, September 19, 2018. https://www.firehouse.com/operations-training/wildland/news/21023220/experts-question-success-of-ca-wildfire-strategy-firefighters.

Kuwada, Robert. "Oak Fire Live Updates: 'Extreme' Wildfire Surpasses 15,500 Acres, Crews Race to Halt Spread." AOL, July 24, 2022. https://www.aol.com/oak-fire-live-updates-massive-031103963.html.

Lin, Rong Gong, II, and Maria L. La Ganga. "They Thought They'd Die Trapped in a Parking Lot." *Los Angeles Times*, December 2, 2018. https://www.latimes.com/local/lanow/la-me-ln-paradise-survivors-20181202-htmlstory.html.

"Listos CA." California State Assembly. Accessed June 29, 2023. https://aem.assembly.ca.gov/listos-ca.

Lundeberg, Steve. "Huge Forest Fires Don't Cause Living Trees to Release Much Carbon, OSU Research Show." Oregon State University, March 14, 2022. https://today.oregonstate.edu/news/huge-forest-fires-don't-cause-living-trees-release-much-carbon-osu-research-shows.

McKay, Dan. "New Mexico's Largest Wildfire: Devastation Lingers One Year since Spark That Lit Hermits Peak Blaze." *Albuquerque Journal*. Updated June 7, 2023. https://www.abqjournal.com/2588273/hermits-peak-calf-canyon-wildfire-new-mexico-one-year-later-devastation-lingers.html.

Mistry, Jayalaxshmi. "Amazon Fires: Indigenous People Show Fire Can Be Used Sustainably." Conversation, August 29, 2019. https://theconversation.com/amazon-fires-indigenous-people-show-fire-can-be-used-sustainably-122493.

Moore, Andrew. "Climate Change Is Making Wildfires Worse—Here's How." College of Natural Resources News, North Carolina State University, August 29, 2022. https://cnr.ncsu.edu/news/2022/08/climate-change-wildfires-explained.

Morrison, Jim. "An Ancient People with a Modern Climate Plan." *Washington Post*, November 24, 2020. https://www.washingtonpost.com/climate-solutions/2020/11/24/native-americans-climate-change-swinomish/.

Morrow, Rory. "What Causes a Fire Tornado?" Your Weather, April 9, 2021. https://www.yourweather.co.uk/news/trending/what-causes-a-fire-tornado-weather-video-wildfire.html.

Mott, Nick. "Scientists Are Learning More about Fire Tornadoes, the Spinning Funnels of Flame." National Public Radio, August 23, 2021. https://www.npr.org/2021/08/23/1029638870/fire-tornadoes-scientists-funnels-flames.

Nyce, Caroline Mimbs. "Those Sequoias Didn't Just Get Lucky." *Atlantic*, July 14, 2022. https://www.theatlantic.com/ideas/archive/2022/07/yosemites-washburn-fire-sequoias/670520.

"Oak Fire: Full Containment Expected by Wednesday, CAL FIRE Says." ABC 30 Action News, August 10, 2022. https://abc30.com/mariposa-county-oak-fire-sierra-national-forest-containment/12114429.

Popovich, Nadja. "See How the Dixie Fire Created Its Own Weather." *New York Times*, October 20, 2021. https://www.nytimes.com/interactive/2021/10/19/climate/dixie-fire-storm-clouds-weather.html.

Pyne, Stephen J. "Vignettes of Primitive America: The Leopold Report and Fire Policy." *Forest History Today* (Spring 2017): 12–18.

Ragland, Gigi. "Public Lands Transformed: Inside Parks' Wildfire Recovery." *Sierra*, July 14, 2021. https://www.sierraclub.org/sierra/public-lands-transformed-inside-parks-wildfire-recovery.

Randall, Brianna. "The Great Plains Prairie Needs Fire to Survive. These Ranchers Are Bringing It Back." *National Geographic*, May 13, 2021. https://www.nationalgeographic.com/environment/article/great-plains-prairie-needs-fire-to-survive-these-ranchers-are-bringing-it-back.

Ray, Kelsey. "Is Aerial Firefighting Worth It?" *High Country News*, August 3, 2015. https://www.hcn.org/issues/47.13/after-a-record-setting-wildfire-a-washington-county-prepares-for-the-next-one/the-cost-benefit-analysis-of-aerial-firefighting.

Renick, Hillary. "Fire, Forests, and Our Lands: An Indigenous Ecological Perspective." First Nations Development Institute, March 16, 2020. https://nonprofitquarterly.org/fire-forests-and-our-lands-an-indigenous-ecological-perspective.

Robbins, Margo. "What TREX Has Meant to One Fire Adapted Culture." Fire Adapted Communities Learning Network, June 28, 2016. https://fireadaptednetwork.org/what-trex-has-meant-to-one-fire-adapted-culture.

Rott, Nathan. "Fire Ecologists Say More Fires Should Be Left to Burn. So Why Aren't They?" *All Things Considered*, National Public Radio, September 27, 2018. https://www.npr.org/2018/09/27/649649316/fire-ecologists-say-more-fires-should-be-left-to-burn-so-why-arent-they.

Santos, Fernanda, and Jack Healy. "A Painful Mix of Fire, Wind and Questions." *New York Times*, July 6, 2013. https://www.nytimes.com/2013/07/07/us/a-painful-mix-of-fire-wind-and-questions.html.

Schwartz, John. "Overlooked No More: Eunice Foote, Climate Scientist Lost to History." *New York Times*, April 27, 2020. https://www.nytimes.com/2020/04/21/obituaries/eunice-foote-overlooked.html.

Smith, Hayley. "Wildfire Burn Areas in California Are Growing Ever Larger Due to Greenhouse Gas Emissions." AOL, June 14, 2023. https://www.aol.com/news/wildfire-burn-areas-california-growing-120024098.html.

Spanne, Autumn. "We're Dumping Loads of Retardant Chemicals to Fight Wildfires. What Does It Mean for Wildlife?" *Environmental Health News*, September 27, 2021. https://www.ehn.org/fire-retardant-spray-wildfire-wildlife-2655069755.html.

Spencer, Christian. "Wildfires Can Actually Create Their Own Weather. Here's How." *Hill*, July 21, 2021. https://thehill.com/changing-america/sustainability/environment/564216-wildfires-can-actually-create-their-own-weather.

Sten, Michaela. "Fire-Adapted: Plants and Animals Rely on Wildfires for Resilient Ecosystems." Defenders of Wildlife, July 12, 2020. https://defenders.org/blog/2020/07/fire-adapted-plants-and-animals-rely-wildfires-resilient-ecosystems.

"Swinomish Climate Change Initiative Climate Adaption Action Plan." Swinomish Indian Tribal Community, October 2010. https://swinomish-nsn.gov/media/54202/swin_cr_2010_01_ccadaptationplan.pdf.

Tarnowski, Stan. *Firefighting in the 21st Century: Where Tradition Meets Technology*. Seattle: Amazon Digital Services—KDP Print US, 2020.

"10 Tips to Prevent Wildfires." US Department of the Interior, May 15, 2023. https://www.doi.gov/blog/10-tips-prevent-wildfires.

Tidwell, Tom. "Big Burn Centennial Commemoration." Transcript of speech given in Boise, Idaho, USDA, May 22, 2010. https://www.fs.usda.gov/speeches/thinking-mountain-about-fire.

Tobias, Jimmy. "Stop with the 'Catastrophic Wildfire' Scare Tactics." *Pacific Standard*, August 15, 2017. https://psmag.com/environment/a-catastrophic-scare-tactic.

Tripp, Bill. "Our Land Was Taken. But We Still Hold the Knowledge of How to Stop Mega-Fires." *Guardian* (US edition), September 16, 2020. https://www.theguardian.com/commentisfree/2020/sep/16/california-wildfires-cultural-burns-indigenous-people.

Turner, Monica G. "30 Years Later: Yellowstone's 1988 Fires Revealed Resilience of Forests." Treesource, September 3, 2018. https://treesource.org/news/lands/yellowstone-fires.

United Nations Environment Programme. *Spreading Like Wildfire: The Rising Threat of Extraordinary Landscape Fires*. Nairobi, Kenya: United Nations Environment Programme, 2022.

"What Is Fire Retardant & How Does It Work?" 10 Tanker, January 25, 2021. https://www.10tanker.com/post/what-is-fire-retardant-how-does-it-work.

"Why Wildfire Smoke Is a Health Concern." United States Environmental Protection Agency. Updated October 20, 2022. https://www.epa.gov/wildfire-smoke-course/why-wildfire-smoke-health-concern.

Wigglesworth, Alex. "Aerial Fire Retardant Drops Are Attacked as Ineffective and Environmentally Harmful," *Los Angeles Times*. Updated March 29, 2023. https://www.latimes.com/california/story/2023-03-29/u-s-forest-service-defends-use-of-pink-wildfire-retardant.

———. "Forest Service Resumes Prescribed Fire Program, but Some Fear New Rules Will Delay Projects." *Los Angeles Times*, September 13, 2022. https://www.latimes.com/california/story/2022-09-13/forest-service-resumes-prescribed-burning.

———. "Two California Fires in the Sierra Nevada Have Very Different Outcomes. Why?" *Los Angeles Times*, July 30, 2022. https://www.latimes.com/california/story/2022-07-30/why-two-california-wildfires-had-very-different-outcomes.

"Wildfires Rage in Western Canada." National Environmental Satellite, Data, and Information Service, May 11, 2023. https://www.nesdis.noaa.gov/news/wildfires-rage-western-canada.

"Wildfire Statistics." Congressional Research Service, March 1, 2023. https://crsreports.congress.gov/product/pdf/IF/IF10244.

Wolfe, Deborah. "Who Are Climate Refugees—and How Can We Help Them?" World Vision, November 2, 2022. https://www.worldvision.ca/stories/climate-change/who-are-climate-refugees-and-how-can-we-help.

FURTHER INFORMATION

Books

Collard, Sneed B. *Fire Birds: Valuing Natural Wildfires and Burned Forests*. Missoula, MT: Bucking Horse Books, 2015.
This short book explores the relationship between forest fires and the plant and animal species that depend on fire for their well-being.

Cottrell, William H., Jr. *The Book of Fire*. Missoula, MT: Mountain, 2004.
Illustrated with colorful graphics, this book covers the chemistry of fire and the factors affecting wildfire behavior.

Hopkinson, Deborah. *The Deadliest Fires Then and Now*. New York: Scholastic Focus, 2022.
This title traces the history of the most destructive fires in US history from the 1871 fire at Peshtigo, Wisconsin, to high-intensity fires driven by climate change in the twenty-first century.

Jensen, Einar. *Ancient Fire, Modern Fire: Understanding and Living with Our Friend and Foe*. Masonville, CO: PixyJack, 2016.
Written by a firefighter, historian, and safety educator, this book provides a history of science, ancient myths about the origin of fire, guidelines for dealing with fire, and a list of fire education resources.

Philbrick, Rodman. *Wildfire: A Novel*. New York: Blue Sky, 2019.
Surrounded by flames, Sam and Delphy must summon all their courage and strength to escape from a wildfire in this novel by a Newbery Honor author. The back matter includes material on wildfires.

Rhodes, Jewell Parker. *Paradise on Fire*. New York: Little, Brown, 2021.
In this award-winning novel, Addy uses her wilderness skills and instincts to lead her friends to safety. Winner of the Green Earth Book Award and the Black Caucus of the American Library Association (BCALA) Best of the Best Book, 2021.

Silverstein, Alvin, Virginia Silverstein, and Laura Silverstein Nunn. *Wildfires: The Science behind Raging Infernos*. Berkeley Heights, NJ: Enslow, 2010.
The authors discuss the causes of wildfires, efforts to contain them, and ways in which scientists study them.

Films

Elemental: Reimagine Wildfire. Written by Ralph Bloemers and Trip Jennings. Directed by Trip Jennings. Portland, OR: Balance Media, 2023.
This comprehensive documentary covers the harrowing community escape from the Camp Fire in Paradise, California, scientific research into fire, Indigenous burning practices, and climate change.

Era of Megafires. A Multimedia Learning Experience. Wenatchee, WA: North Forty Productions, 2018.
Noted ecologist Paul Hessburg discusses the growing frequency of megafires, what causes them, and how they can be mitigated. The film can be viewed at https://eraofmegafires.com.

Fire Wars. Written by Rushmore DeNooyer, Larry Engel, and Judith Vecchione. Directed by Larry Engel and Kirk Wolfinger. *NOVA*, first aired May 7, 2002.
This episode of the PBS science series focuses on smoke jumpers and hotshots responding to wildfires during the especially fearsome fire season of 2000.

Only the Brave. Screenplay by Ken Nolan and Eric Warren Singer. Directed by Joseph Kosinski. Culver City, CA: Columbia Pictures, 2017.
This film tells the tragic story of the Granite Mountain Hotshots who died at the Yarnell Hill Fire.

Rebuilding Paradise. Directed by Ron Howard. Washington, DC: National Geographic Documentary Films, 2020.
In this documentary, the people of Paradise, California, courageously seek to rebuild their town one year after it was destroyed in one of the worst fires in California's history.

Wilder Than Wild: Fire, Forests, and the Future. Written by Stephen Most. Directed and narrated by Kevin White. San Francisco: Filmmakers Collaborative SF, 2018.
This film discusses the way the accumulation of fuel in landscapes and climate change have led to megafires, covers the importance of prescribed burns, depicts the fire traditions of a California tribe, and much more.

Websites

Division of Wildland Fire Management (US Department of the Interior: Indian Affairs)
https://www.bia.gov/bia/ots/dwfm
This website presents "Fast Facts" about wildfires on Indigenous lands and links to services provided to tribal nations.

Fire: National Park Service
https://www.nps.gov/subjects/fire/index.htm
The National Park Service provides links on fire seasons, fire preparedness, fire scientists, wildland fire, safety resources, and other topics.

Great Basin Smokejumpers
https://www.nifc.gov/about-us/what-is-nifc/smokejumpers
Learn what it means to be a smoke jumper, and explore links to more information on the history and work of the National Interagency Fire Center.

Smokey Bear
https://www.smokeybear.com
Smokey Bear's message has expanded well beyond his traditional motto. This website includes links to the benefits of fire, fire-dependent ecosystems, prescribed fire, fire safety, and much more.

US Forest Service: Managing Fire
https://www.fs.usda.gov/science-technology/fire
This Forest Service website contains general information on fires as well as links to material on fire research, aviation technology, firefighting tools, fire crews on the ground and in the air, fire forecasting, and more.

The World on Fire
https://www.pbs.org/wgbh/nova/fire/world.html
This website allows you to explore fire around the world through interactive global fire maps for 2000, an especially severe fire year around the world.

INDEX

PHOTO ACKNOWLEDGMENTS

Image credits: AP Photo/Gabrielle Lurie/San Francisco Chronicle, p. 5; Penitentes/Wikimedia Commons (CC BY-SA 4.0), p. 7; iStock/Getty Images, p. 8; National Park Service, p. 11; Ed Reschke/Getty Images, p. 12; Charles Melton/Alamy, p. 14; Philip Schubert/Shutterstock, p. 16; Agami Photo Agency/Shutterstock, p. 18; Danita Delimont/Alamy, p. 20; VectorMine/Shutterstock, p. 24; Jason I/Shutterstock, p. 28; anatoliy_gleb/Shutterstock, p. 29; AP Photo/David Goldman, p. 31, 34; Courtesy of MBCI, p. 32; Fairfax Media/Getty Images, p. 37; John R Kruel/Independent Picture Service, p. 38–39; Library of Congress, p. 42; Rick Shu/500px/Getty Images, p. 44; S.J. Photography/Shutterstock, p. 47; Buyenlarge/Getty Images, p. 48; MShieldsPhotos/Alamy, p. 51; Lucky-photographer/Shutterstock, p. 53; Wirestock Creators/Shutterstock, p. 55; Selcuk Acar/Anadolu Agency/Getty Images, p. 58; ESA (Contains modified Copernicus Sentinel data 2023), p. 61; Pictorial Press Ltd/Alamy, p. 63; Majority World CIC/Alamy, p. 65; Moritz et al. 2012/Wikimedia Commons (CC BY-SA 4.0), p. 66; Daria Nipot/Shutterstock, p. 69; HECTOR MATA/AFP/Getty Images, p. 72; Markiss Smith, p. 73; Brook Mitchell/Getty Images, p. 75; EndeavorMoorePhotography/Shutterstock, p. 77; USFS Photo/Alamy, p. 79; Courtesy of the NOAA, p. 83; RooM the Agency/Alamy, p. 84; Craig Larcom/Alamy, p. 85; Brian van der Brug/Los Angeles Times/Getty Images, p. 89; Lucas Ninno/Getty Images, p. 90; Kirstin Adams-Bimson/Shutterstock, p. 92; Jaden Schaul/Shutterstock, p. 96; Helen H. Richardson/The Denver Post/Getty Images, p. 99; Philip Pacheco/Bloomberg/Getty Images, p. 101; USDA Forest Service, p. 106; Amit Basu Photography/Getty Images, p. 109; Carlos Avila Gonzalez/The San Francisco Chronicle/Getty Images, p. 111; George Rose/Getty Images, p. 114.

Design elements: pupahava/Shutterstock; getgg/Shutterstock; Peter Yost/Unsplash.

Cover: Christian Roberts-Olsen/Shutterstock.

ABOUT THE AUTHORS

Ferin Davis Anderson is an environmental scientist and an enrolled citizen of the Turtle Mountain Band of Chippewa/Ojibwe/Anishinaabe/Mitchifs in North Dakota. She works as the Supervisor of Environmental Sciences for the Shakopee Mdewakanton Sioux Community's Land and Natural Resources Department where she is responsible for stewarding and restoring natural areas for the SMSC. Anderson weaves traditional knowledge and western science together to make more holistic management decisions, including using fire as an ecological and cultural tool to achieve beneficial and healing outcomes. Witnessing Indigenous people revitalize and reconnect with this practice has been one of the greatest gifts of her career.

Stephanie Sammartino McPherson wrote her first children's story in college. She enjoyed the process so much that she's never stopped writing. A former teacher and freelance newspaper writer, she has written more than thirty books and numerous magazine stories. Her recent books include *Hothouse Earth: The Climate Crisis and the Importance of Carbon Neutrality*, winner of the Green Earth Book Award for young adult nonfiction, and *Breakthrough: Katalin Karikó and the mRNA Vaccine*. McPherson and her husband, Richard, live in Virginia.